THEY CAME TO MURRAMARANG

A History of Murramarang,
Kioloa and Bawley Point

THEY CAME TO MURRAMARANG

A History of Murramarang, Kioloa and Bawley Point

BRUCE HAMON
Edited by Alastair Greig and Sue Feary

PRESS

Published by ANU Press
The Australian National University
Acton ACT 2601, Australia
Email: anupress@anu.edu.au
This title is also available online at http://press.anu.edu.au

National Library of Australia Cataloguing-in-Publication entry

Creator: Hamon, B. V., author.

Title: They came to Murramarang : a history of Murramarang, Kioloa and Bawley Point / Bruce Hamon ; edited by Alastair Greig, Sue Feary.

Edition: Revised edition.

ISBN: 9781925022742 (paperback) 9781925022759 (ebook)

Subjects: Murramarang (N.S.W.)--History.
Kioloa (N.S.W.)--History.
Bawley Point (N.S.W.)--History.

Other Creators/Contributors:
Greig, Alastair Whyte, 1960- editor.
Feary, Sue, editor.

Dewey Number: 994.47

All rights reserved. No part of this publication may be reproduced, stored in a retrieval system or transmitted in any form or by any means, electronic, mechanical, photocopying or otherwise, without the prior permission of the publisher.

Cover design and layout by ANU Press

Cover illustration: North Beach, Bawley Point, from near the mouth of Willinga Lake. Watercolour by Alma Hamon, c. 1920.

First edition published © 1994 Centre for Resource and Environmental Studies, The Australian National University

This edition © 2015 ANU Press

CONTENTS

List of maps, figures and tables vii
Acknowledgements xi
About the editors xiii
Unit conversions xv
Introduction to the new edition xvii
    Alastair Greig
Peopling the landscape xxvii
    Sue Feary
Author's preface xxxiii
Locality map and notes xxxv
1.   Pre-settlement 1
2.   Settlement at Murramarang 7
3.   The Evans era 23
4.   Timber! 35
5.   Turn of the century 53
6.   Transport: Ships and roads 71
7.   Bawley Point in the 1920s 87
8.   The 1920s and 1930s 113
9.   Recent developments 135
Epilogue: Murramarang in the early twenty-first century 145
    Alastair Greig and Sue Feary
Index 153

LIST OF MAPS, FIGURES AND TABLES

Maps

Map 1: Locality map xxxiv

Figures

Figure 1: Bruce Hamon aged 15, with Bobby the cat xx

Figure 2: Bruce on a bushwalk, with a White-eared Honeyeater removing his hair for nesting material xxi

Figure 3: Bruce Hamon in Sydney, 1972 xxii

Figure 4: Bruce Hamon at Minnamurra, c. 1995 xxv

Figure 5: Aboriginal sites recorded in the Murramarang area in 2014 xxix

Figure 6: Murramarang from Brush Island, c. 1955, before dune stabilisation . . . 3

Figure 7: Murramarang House 18

Figure 8: Wall construction, Murramarang House 19

Figure 9: Plan of the Village of Kioloa, 1843 21

Figure 10: John Evans II, c. 1900 27

Figure 11: Neil Evans and bullock team, c. 1939 29

Figure 12: Windsor Evans felling a tree, 1952 31

Figure 13: McKenzie's sawmill, Kioloa, probably before the 1916 fire 37

Figure 14: McKenzie's sawmill, Kioloa, c. 1920, with ship moored for loading . . 38

Figure 15: Bawley Point sawmill, c. 1915 40

Figure 16: Mill lease at Bawley Point 41

Figure 17: Horse team pulling logs on the tramline, Kioloa 42

Figure 18: Horse team led by 'old Prince' crossing tramline bridge
over Willinga Lake, c. 1914 43

Figure 19: Workers and children at Bawley Point sawmill, c. 1915 44

Figure 20: Method of loading timber, Bawley Point 46

Figure 21: Bawley Point mill site, 1976 52

Figure 22: Kioloa school house being relocated closer to The Avenue 55

Figure 23: Termeil School, on Old Schoolhouse Road, off Monkey
Mountain Road. 56

Figure 24: The Hamon's house, which also served as the Bawley Point
Telephone Office. 61

Figure 25: Kioloa rugby football team, c. 1910 68

Figure 26: *Athol Star* wrecked on Bull Pup Beach, c. 1950. 76

Figure 27: *Northern Firth* wrecked on Brush Island, February 1932. 77

Figure 28: *Douglas Mawson*, built at Bawley Point, launched 11 April 1914 . . . 78

Figure 29: *Douglas Mawson* under construction, Bawley Point, 1913. 79

Figure 30: Old coach road, 1988 82

Figure 31: Collins' household goods being moved from Taralga
to Willinga, 1919. 83

Figure 32: Wooden bridge over Willinga Lake, c. 1960 85

Figure 33: The Hamon's cottage and telephone office c. 1930 89

Figure 34: Reg (left) and Innes Collins and their parents, Kioloa, c. 1932. 91

Figure 35: Walter Scott at Willinga, probably c. 1930 92

Figure 36: Alma Hamon and 'Mit', c. 1930 95

Figure 37: Bawley Point c. 1927, after the mill fire 96

Figure 38: Rodney Ellis and Charles Parsons with jewfish,
Bawley Point, 1934 99

Figure 39: Mary (May or Broda) Reynolds and Henry Reynolds,
Bawley Point, c. 1930 106

Figure 40: Moving two rooms of one of the mill cottages at Bawley Point
to a site near the north end of Bawley Point Beach, c. 1925. 107

Figure 41: Ralph Johnston's memorial to his pets, Johnston Street,
Bawley Point 109

LIST OF FIGURES, MAPS AND TABLES

Figure 42: Mill workers' cottages, O'Hara Head, Kioloa, c. 1912. 115

Figure 43: The Avenue, Kioloa, c. 1925 116

Figure 44: Joy London's house, Kioloa, c. 1950 118

Figure 45: Hum Moore and the 32-volt property generator, 1947 119

Figure 46: Joy London with Bimbo 120

Figure 47: 'New' guest house, Bawley Point, mid-to-late 1930s 122

Figure 48: Bawley Point Guest House before its closure in 2001. 123

Figure 49: Gwen Kellond, Pat Kellond (in front of Gwen), Bobbie Moore, Mrs George Moore, Marie Kellond, Clarrie Kellond. Kioloa Beach, c. 1925. 124

Figure 50: Walter Scott, mailman, Kioloa–Termeil, c. 1930 131

Figure 51: Bawley Point Beach, c. 1934. 132

Figure 52: Old crane mill at Bawley Point. This picture was taken around 1950, almost 30 years after the mill was destroyed. 133

Figure 53: Transfer of title to the Edith and Joy London Foundation property from Miss Joy London to The Australian National University, 1 March 1975 137

Figure 54: Entrance to the Edith and Joy London Foundation, The Australian National University, Kioloa, before the renovation of the cottages on The Avenue. 138

Figure 55: The Avenue, Kioloa, 1976 140

Figure 56: Baxter's sawmill, Termeil, 2015. 141

Tables

Table 1: Landowners, 1829–1930, Bawley Point–Murramarang–Kioloa 9

Table 2: Occupation and civil status of residents of Murramarang (1841 Census) 16

Table 3: Simplified Evans family tree 25

ACKNOWLEDGEMENTS

The late H. J. Gibbney, who had started the project, and whose notes and interview files have been invaluable.

Joy London, who maintained a lively interest throughout.

Dorothy Watts and Lorna Froude contributed in many ways, especially with interview transcripts and results of literature searches, and many pleasant and helpful discussions on the project.

Eric Simpson, Peter Scheele, Clarrie Rogerson and Jack Wallace were particularly helpful for the chapter on timber.

Reg and Innes Collins, the late Mrs Isabel Vider, and the late Neil Evans have contributed much over the years.

Joanne Ewin and Cathy Dunn have helped greatly to set the wider background.

Alex McAndrew provided much enthusiasm and input.

John Oliver helped with his photographic skills.

Bob Sneddon provided some useful references.

Robert Hyslop helped with editorial advice.

Mrs N. Guy and Mrs Jean Brierley.

Olive Baxter, Ena Bevan, Clarice Egan, Gwen Illek, Grace Jarman, Marie McClung, Heather Sharp, Edna Veith, Aileen Wilford.

Staff of the following institutions have been very helpful: Archives Authority of NSW; Australian Archives, Sydney; Department of Conservation and Land Management, Sydney; National Library, Canberra; Shoalhaven City Council; State Library of NSW.

Acknowledgements for the second edition

Alastair Greig and Sue Feary are indebted to Margaret Hamon for her generous time and effort in helping prepare this second edition. Not only did Margaret assist with interviews and the search for illustrations, she also read through and commented upon the new edition. The Edith and Joy London Foundation of The Australian National University also provided invaluable assistance and encouragement. Comments from two anonymous referees were also gratefully received. Finally, the editors are very grateful to the ANU Publication Subsidy Committee's generous financial assistance for copy editing.

ABOUT THE EDITORS

Dr Alastair Greig is a Reader in Sociology at The Australian National University. His association with the Murramarang area sprang from his parents' decision to locate the family caravan at Pretty Beach. Since residential vans were removed from the site, early in the new millennium, Alastair has been a member of ANU Kioloa Advisory Board. His books include *The Australian Way of Life* (2013), *Challenging Global Inequality* (2007), *Inequality in Australia* (2003) and *The Stuff Dreams Are Made Of* (1995). He is the recipient of numerous national and ANU teaching awards, as well as, most recently, the Chancellor's Award for Outstanding Contribution to the Campus Community.

Dr Sue Feary is an archaeologist and retired national park manager who has worked with South Coast Aboriginal people for many years, recording and protecting their cultural heritage. Her special interest is the history of Aboriginal involvement in the forest sector, from employment in the timber history to traditional approaches to caring for forest country. She has a very long association with Murramarang, having established the first interpretive walking trail on Murramarang Aboriginal Area in 1990, while employed by the NSW National Parks and Wildlife Service. She stayed often at the Kioloa field studies centre as an ANU archaeology undergraduate in the 1980s, and again in the 2000s, when she tutored in the Fenner School and ran fieldtrips as part of a first-year course on resources, environment and society.

UNIT CONVERSIONS

1 acre = 0.41 ha

1 rod = 5.03 m

1 foot = 0.30 m

1 mile = 1.61 km

12 pence = 1 shilling

1 shilling = 10 cents

1 pound = $2.00

1 horsepower = 746 watts

1 gallon = 4.55 litres

1 superficial foot (or 'super') is a measure of volume of timber, equal to one-twelfth of a cubic foot, or 0.002 m^3.

INTRODUCTION TO THE NEW EDITION
Alastair Greig

The significance of *They Came to Murramarang*

They Came to Murramarang was first published in 1994, providing the New South Wales South Coast villages of Bawley Point, Kioloa and the surrounding area with an authoritative history from colonial settlement through to the contemporary era. High demand for the book led to subsequent reprints in 1997 and 2001. Ongoing requests for reprints attest to its popularity, with readers ranging from residents within the district and holiday makers discovering the beauty of the area, to academics interested in the history of this once isolated part of the South Coast.

In considering another reprint, two decades after its initial release, the author Bruce Hamon was aware that the region has experienced considerable development since the early 1990s and it is appropriate to consider these changes. Bruce was also aware of research conducted into particular historical episodes associated with the region since the original publication, which augments his account presented in *They Came to Murramarang*. Furthermore, he felt that the original text provided only a brief glimpse into the rich story of the Indigenous custodians of the country, even though the book presented a fascinating account of early colonial frontier conflict. In incorporating these changes and discoveries, Bruce sought my assistance, along with that of Dr Sue Feary, an archaeologist with extensive knowledge of Indigenous history and environmental policy in the region. Bruce passed away in August 2014 before the book went to print.

The most difficult dilemma in considering how to incorporate these changes into a new edition was that the book itself has become part of the history of Murramarang. The book remains the only comprehensive account of the region. This was partly due to the diligent archival efforts of the author. More importantly, Bruce was able to write the history from a unique position of authority because his family were early settlers in the region and he himself grew up within the small settlement of Bawley Point between 1918 and 1930. Under circumstances where archival records and archaeological evidence are sparse, the testimonies of local people become even more significant. Bruce not only had access to such testimonies, but was also part of the community's history, having lived through its transformation from the timber age to the present.

Given the unique position of the author, no book can surpass *They Came to Murramarang* as a historical record of the area. This new edition has remained mindful of Bruce's legacy, and Sue and I have ensured that readers have full access to his own words.

The life of the author[1]

Bruce provided rich insight into his early life in Chapter 7, 'Bawley Point in the 1920s', and these reminiscences remain the most vivid we possess of life in the region towards the end of the timber-milling era. His connections with the region, however, can be traced back to his great-grandparents on both sides, who settled in Milton in the 1850s. When Bruce's parents, Les and Alma, were expecting Bruce's arrival — he was born on 11 August 1917 — his mother was sent to Sydney, where they both remained during Bruce's first year. The family then moved to Bawley Point, where his father was a mill hand at Guy's timber mill.

After the mill burned down in April 1922, Bruce's father was retained in the capacity of a load tally clerk at Bawley Point, as a timber mill still operated at Flat Rock near Monkey Mountain Road north of Termeil. The population of Bawley Point by then had been reduced to around a dozen households.

At the age of seven, Bruce was enrolled at Murramarang School, before its closure forced Bruce's mother — who was determined that Bruce advance his education as far as possible — to transfer him to Termeil School when he was 11 years old.

---

[1] In writing this section, I drew extensively on two interviews conducted with Bruce Hamon and Margaret Hamon at Bruce's home in Bawley Point in July and August 2012. I also consulted a memoir Bruce wrote detailing his professional career, entitled *My Working Life*. Additional support was also provided by Nicholas Steinmetz and Bruce's work colleagues at CSIRO, including Stuart Godfrey, George Cresswell, John Church, Alan Pearce, George Veronis, and Ian Jones.

He traversed the 10-kilometre daily journey on his pony, Titch. Even though this westerly journey became familiar, he rarely ever ventured five kilometres south to the village of Kioloa. Today they are considered twin villages. Given the isolation of Bawley Point during this time, Bruce spent much of his childhood exploring the coastal and marine environment. He vividly recalled his interest in the visit of a team of marine surveyors to Bawley Point.

At the age of 13, Bruce received a bursary to attend St Patrick's College in Goulburn where he boarded for four years. During his time there, his mother began operating the Bawley Point Guest House. His parents had already been taking in guests ever since his mother visited a Sydney optometrist, Dr Blaxland, who subsequently visited Bawley Point, and then informed others of this tranquil spot and the convivial local hospitality. Word of mouth was the only advertising the Hamon's business required. Bruce's parents purchased land and his father, with the help of Frank Carriage (described by Bruce as a 'fisherman, builder, jack-of-all-trades'), built the more commodious guest house. The house still stands on Johnston Street in Bawley Point, an extension of Murramarang Road, heading north towards Willinga Lake, although it closed as a guest house in 2001. The guest house had its own orchard, vegetable gardens and chicken house, while a tennis court and motel-style units were later added.

During his schooling in Goulburn, Bruce would return to Bawley Point during school holidays. Most of the visitors at the guest house came from Sydney. One keen fisherman, the head of electrical engineering at University of Sydney, Professor John Madsen (knighted in 1954), encouraged Bruce to consider engineering at university. The young Bruce thought engineers drove steam trains.

Bruce was accepted into Sydney University and studied electrical engineering for four years, followed by an additional year of mathematics and physics. In 1941, his technical skills were in high demand as a result of the war and he began his career-long association with the CSIRO by choosing to join the National Standards Laboratory. He soon became adept at designing precision resistors that improved the accuracy of measurements. Throughout his career, Bruce published some 70 papers in various journals such as *The Journal of Scientific Instruments*. His renown became international, and one Canadian company continues to advertise 'Hamon Type Resistance Transfer Standards'.

Figure 1: Bruce Hamon aged 15, with Bobby the cat.
Source: Margaret Hamon.

Bruce also participated in various wartime projects, including one associated with improving the range accuracy of coastal defence guns. This included an assignment to Britain between June 1943 and February 1944. On his first international flight, to San Francisco, his seating allocation consisted of mailbags. On his return to Sydney, he was involved in projects de-gaussing ships, limiting their risk to magnetic mines.

After the war, Bruce continued his work on precision instruments, venturing into the design of oceanographic electronic devices. He also led a research team calibrating instruments for measuring salinity, temperature and depth. These professional duties drew him back to his childhood fascination with coastal and marine environments. Eventually, this path led him to join the CSIRO's Division of Fisheries at Cronulla, in February 1957, and he spent the following year on a UNESCO Fellowship in Marine Science at Britain's National Institute of Oceanography, in the company of his wife, Anne, and daughter, Margaret. On his return to Australia, Bruce became interested in currents, tides and waves, and he was credited with 'discovering' the 'continental shelf wave' (although, modestly, Bruce observes that they are mentioned in *The Royal Society Philosophical Transactions* of June 1665). Much of his scientific work at the CSIRO during the 1960s and 1970s was devoted to oceanographic observations of the eastern coast of Australia, the same coast he had fished from at isolated Bawley Point.

Figure 2: Bruce on a bushwalk, with a White-eared Honeyeater removing his hair for nesting material.
Source: Margaret Hamon.

He retired from the CSIRO in August 1979 and became an Honorary Associate at the Marine Studies Centre at Sydney University, the university where his initial training commenced. He remained an active researcher, specialising in time-series data for tides and sea levels. He stated that: 'I have enjoyed my working life. I enjoyed the freedom to choose projects.' Testimonies from those who Bruce worked with or supervised confirm that he commanded enormous respect by allowing his team latitude in pursuing their interests and balancing work with non-work life. Through this approach, Bruce built a work culture characterised by trust, loyalty and mutual respect. He has been acclaimed as the father of physical oceanography in Australia.

His retirement allowed him to pursue his other interests, including fishing, bird-watching, astronomy and woodwork. He put his woodworking skills to good use making many wooden items for Technical Aids for the Disabled. Having lived at Caringbah since 1957, Bruce moved back to Bawley Point in June 2005. Surrounded by family members and friends, Bruce was able to remain living independently at Bawley Point until March 2013, when he moved to IRT Crown Gardens at Batemans Bay. He passed away peacefully on 24 August 2014.

Figure 3: Bruce Hamon (2nd on left) holding a replica of the Hamon Transfer Standard presented to him by the American Ambassador, Walter L. Rice (on right), at the opening of the Scientific Instrumentation Exhibition at the United States Trade Centre, Sydney, 14 August 1972.
Source: Margaret Hamon. Photographers: John Ciarotto and Tessa Guilfoyle.

INTRODUCTION TO THE NEW EDITION

Writing *They Came to Murramarang*[2]

While Bruce enjoyed the freedom to choose research projects throughout his life, one can only wonder why he chose to turn from his expertise in precision measurement towards the local history of an isolated region where only rudimentary records existed. *They Came To Murramarang* is one of the most challenging projects Bruce chose in his research career. Yet readers of the history quickly come to admire the way in which the author used a wide range of research material — from census data to electoral rolls, from early settler journals to newspaper reports, and from interviews to personal recollection — to present a compelling narrative of how a set of small isolated communities battled to connect themselves with a wider world that itself had created — and continually transformed — the small communities. This narrative of isolation and connection ran through Bruce's quest to understand his community.

The road out of Bawley Point was always of particular interest to Bruce, literally and metaphorically. He remembered as a child the stonework at Willinga Lake that marked the Old South Coast Road, built some time before 1837. He used to trace the visible remnants of this road south from Bawley Point, up Durras Mountain and down to Pebbly Beach. His mother, as noted below, painted an image of the stonework at the side of the road in the early 1920s.

He wrote letters to the Royal Australian Historical Society in January 1964 and the Illawarra Historical Society in March 1964 requesting information about when the old coast road was in use and whether it ever carried a coach service. However, neither society could furnish the necessary details. In 1982, after reading George Antill's book, *Settlement in the South: A record of the discovery, exploration and settlement of the Shoalhaven River Basin 1803–1982*, he wrote to the author asking for further information on the road as well as more information on the schools in the Murramarang district. Antill's detailed response only confirmed to Bruce how limited and sketchy the record of the region was. Antill himself camped at Bawley Point with his family around 1930 and recalled the Hamons.

Now retired, Bruce began spending more time exercising his own historical memory and those of others. He wrote notes for his daughter Margaret on his grandmother, Broda Reynolds, who also lived at Bawley Point in the 1920s. In 1983, he also took notes from a conversation about the history of the region with Neil Evans, whose family history in the region went back to the 1850s. Bruce also sought traces of information about Bawley Point and Kioloa before his birth through researching editions of the *Nowra Leader* from 1913 and 1914.

---

2   In writing this section, I am grateful to Bruce Hamon for providing me with a folio containing his correspondence associated with researching and writing *They Came to Murramarang*.

In 1985, Bruce sent an unpublished memoir of life at Bawley Point to Jim Gibbney, who had become the 'official' historian of the Edith and Joy London Foundation when the property was handed over to The Australian National University in 1975. Gibbney, one of Canberra's most renowned historians, resigned from the role in 1977, but responded to Bruce's memoir by complimenting him on 'a readable and useful piece of work, indeed I consider it one of the best things of its type that I have seen in a long professional career'.

Bruce was interested in Gibbney's confession that he had begun to research a history of the area but was eventually forced to abandon the project. He informed Bruce that transcribed interviews existed with locals such as Reg and Innes Collins, Ernie Donovan, Belle Vider and Bill Cullen. Bruce also discovered that Owen Dent, who had taken possession of these materials, was not in a position to continue writing the history. More importantly, Bruce offered his assistance to Lorna Froude and Dorothy Watts, who had also begun writing a history of the district.

At this time, the early 1990s, Bruce was still living in Caringbah, Sutherland shire, and used this opportunity to trawl through the State Library in earnest. Between December 1991 and March 1992, Bruce wrote a series of long letters to Dorothy providing a wealth of information that he had obtained from his research into the *Milton and Ulladulla Times* around the turn of the twentieth century. These letters reveal the value of Bruce's training in precision instruments combined with the mind of a critical historian, always questioning contradiction and searching for explanations of events out of limited material. In a March 1992 letter to Dorothy, he finally summoned the courage to state: 'I should have enough material now to start writing!' His initial interest in the Old South Coast Road had taken him on a much longer journey than he could have anticipated.

Shortly after this, Bruce spoke with Dr Brian Lees, an ANU geographer involved with the Edith and Joy London Foundation, about the possibility of writing the history. In July 1992, he wrote more firmly to Lees, confirming that he was interested in continuing the project — with help from Lorna and Dorothy — and Lees granted him permission to use Gibbney's transcripts. He also outlined the structure of the proposed book, which bore an uncanny resemblance to the final product, and anticipated that the project would take a year.

This proved to be a frenetic year in which Bruce attacked his project with the same stamina and critical questioning that he had devoted to his CSIRO work. Letters were sent around the country with a wide range of requests for documentary assistance and clarification, prefaced with the explanation that he was 'about to start a short history'. He wrote to the CSIRO about rabbits on Brush Island, to a range of different historical societies asking for details about electoral rolls, to record offices about assigned convicts, to academics about wages and conditions, to the National Museum of Australia on particular Indigenous identities, and to experts on shipwrecks. He even found time to warn ANU about the early spread of Bitou Bush at Kioloa.

In the midst of his research, Bruce also rediscovered the watercolour that his mother painted of the stonework on the Old South Coast Road at Willinga Lake. This was found at King House, in rooms used by the Milton-Ulladulla Historical Society. Bruce wrote to the society, seeking permission to use it on the cover of the forthcoming book.

ANU had expressed interest in the book in January 1992, and in August 1993 the ANU Centre for Resources and Environmental Studies agreed to underwrite the costs of publishing it. With the precision that had characterised his professional life, Bruce delivered the manuscript on time, and its publication ensured that it became part of the history of the region.

Figure 4: Bruce Hamon at Minnamurra, c. 1995.
Source: Margaret Hamon.

Changes in this edition

This new edition of *They Came to Murramarang* includes some significant new features while respecting the integrity of the first edition. Readers therefore have access to Bruce's original history in addition to new material that places the original text in perspective.

Any changes Bruce requested have been added to his original endnotes within each chapter, which have been converted to footnotes for this edition. Bruce wanted to retain the artwork that adorned the cover of the original edition, the watercolour of North Beach at Bawley Point painted by his mother Alma around 1920. However, in this edition, the detail gives more prominence to the stonework marking the edge of the road (or dray track) from Murramarang to Milton, built in the 1830s. The text has also been supplemented in this edition with additional photographs held by Margaret Hamon and the Edith and Joy London Foundation.

Apart from these changes, the original text is presented here, contextualised with this introduction. This is followed by a new chapter written by Dr Sue Feary on the Indigenous history of the region. In acknowledgement of their deep and ongoing association with the land, Bruce recognised the need for an introductory chapter describing the history of the original custodians of the Murramarang country. Dr Feary has also inserted explanatory footnotes to Bruce's text, providing readers with further details of the Indigenous regional heritage. In presenting more information about 'the other side of the frontier', Bruce hoped that this second edition would play a modest role in the process of reconciliation. These editorial footnotes at the bottom of the relevant page are distinguished from Bruce's own notes by being marked: '(A.G. and S.F.)'.

At the end of the original text, an epilogue written by Alastair Greig and Sue Feary supplements Bruce's history by describing social, economic and environmental developments in the district during the two decades since the original publication of *They Came to Murramarang*.

PEOPLING THE LANDSCAPE

Sue Feary

Imagine a time, around 20,000 years ago. The landscape of Murramarang and Kioloa looks markedly different. Most noticeable is the absence of the ocean, which is not even visible in the distance, being about 120 metres lower than today and 14 kilometres further out. The climate is cold and dry and ocean water is captured in the massive polar ice caps. In place of the ocean there is a large rolling plain with rocky outcrops, ridges and hills, covered in forest and bush, and providing sustenance for Australia's grazing megafauna — giant kangaroos, wombats and diprotodons.

Around this time, a geological epoch known as the Pleistocene was coming to a close, having commenced around 100,000 years earlier. Around 20,000 years ago the greater Australian continent (Australia, New Guinea and Tasmania) was already occupied by Aboriginal people who had 'island-hopped' from Southeast Asia some 30,000 years earlier when sea levels were at their lowest, although the exact route will probably never be known.[1] Over generations, this founder population fanned out across the continent and, as numbers increased, settlement occurred along what we now call the NSW South Coast. Although rising sea levels may have drowned much of the earliest archaeological evidence, two important sites demonstrate the great antiquity of Aboriginal occupation in the region. The first is a large shell midden at Bass Point, near Kiama, where archaeological excavations conducted in the late 1960s showed human occupation commencing around 17,000 years ago.[2]

---

1   Hiscock, P. *Archaeology of Ancient Australia*, Routledge, London and New York, 2008.
2   Bowdler, S. *Bass Point: the excavation of a southeast Australian shell midden showing cultural and economic change*, BA (Hons), University of Sydney, 1970.

Second, and closer to home, archaeological excavations in the floor of a large sandstone overhang on the southern side of what is now Burrill Lake found that humans had lived there from 21,000 years ago.[3] This archaeological research (conducted more than 40 years ago and mentioned by Bruce in his opening chapter) generated considerable national and international interest because, at the time, it was one of the oldest archaeological sites yet discovered in Australia and seriously challenged existing theories of human origins and dispersal. It put the Antipodes on the world map!

The Burrill Lake rockshelter would have been next to a river flowing out onto the plain, and the archaeological evidence in the lowest levels of the cultural deposits reflect a diet based on terrestrial resources. It is not until the higher and younger deposit levels are reached that marine species appear amongst the food remains, correlating with palaeoenvironmental data showing that the sea reached its current level around 5,000 to 6,000 years ago. Those first generations of Aboriginal Australians must have experienced and adapted to climate change on an unparalleled scale.

In the early 1980s, the National Parks and Wildlife Service (NPWS) covered the floor of the rockshelter with a thick layer of gravel to protect the precious cultural layers underneath.[4] Today the Burrill lake rockshelter is surrounded by houses but it still manages to convey a powerful sense of the past. The rockshelter is situated on a small piece of land owned by the Shoalhaven City Council, who manages it in conjunction with the NSW Office of Environment and Heritage (OEH, formerly NPWS) and local Aboriginal communities. The rockshelter's significance is reflected through its listing in the Shoalhaven Local Environmental Plan and on the State Heritage Register. It remains of cultural significance to Aboriginal people, has historical value as one of the earliest systematic excavations in Australia, and has scientific value, due to its age and its provision of important information on early Aboriginal occupation.

Saltwater people settle in

The archaeological evidence for Pleistocene occupation of the eastern seaboard is sparse, suggesting that population levels were low. But the story is very different following the rise and stabilisation of the ocean at its current level around 5,000 years ago. Rocky headlands, such as O'Hara Head, Murramarang Point and Snapper Point, jutted out over massive rocky shore platforms, and

---

3   Lampert, R. *Burrill Lake and Currarong*, Terra Australis 1: ANU, Canberra, 1971.
4   Snelson, W. and Sullivan, M. 'Barbeques at Burrill Lake? Or, what has been done to restore, protect and manage the Burrill Lake rockshelter site', *Australian Archaeology*, 1982, 15:20–26.

behind them was a network of wetlands, lagoons and coastal lakes. Together with the surrounding forests, they were a bountiful resource to a now fully coastal Aboriginal population. Also created by rising seas were many small offshore islands, which were often important spiritually and as a source of particular foods such as penguins, seals or shearwaters. They may have become inhabited as a result of population pressure on the mainland.[5] Human populations possibly increased in response to the abundance and variety of resources. Archaeological sites become much more numerous after this time, especially around 2,000 years ago, although this may also be partly a function of having had less time to decay.[6]

Figure 5: Aboriginal sites recorded in the Murramarang area in 2014.
Source: NSW Office of Environment and Heritage, Aboriginal heritage database 20/1/2014.

---

5   Sullivan, M. 'Exploitation of off-shore islands along the New South Wales Coastline', *Australian Archaeology*, 1982, 15: 8–19.
6   Lampert, R. and Hughes, P. 'Sea level change and Aboriginal coastal adaptations in southern New South Wales', *Archaeology and Physical Anthropology in Oceania*, 1974, 9:226–235.

The dots in the map in Figure 5 are Aboriginal sites recorded on the OEH database between Bawley Point and Kioloa. While the number and position of dots is partly a function of where people have looked, it also reflects traditional Aboriginal use and occupation of the landscape. Traditional saltwater Aboriginal people probably lived along the coast for much of the year, and the map shows a focus on headlands, perhaps because they had resource-rich rocky platforms below them and provided good vantage points to see schools of fish or advancing hostile tribes. All the headlands extending from Bawley Point down through Murramarang National Park contain shell middens and many have extensive scatters of stone artefacts.

Much of what we know of ancient Aboriginal life comes from a study of these shell middens, where calcium carbonate in the shell preserves organic material such as charcoal from fires, animal bone and occasionally plant remains. The material evidence points to the importance of fish and other marine creatures in the traditional diet. Bones of many different fish species can be found when shell middens are scientifically excavated, giving an indication of species preference and even the time of year that the ancient fishers were at work. Also present may be fishhooks made from abalone and turbo shell honed to shape with stone files, and stone points, once attached to five-pronged fishing spears made from specially selected wood. Whale and seal bones, such as those in the Murramarang Point midden, indicate opportunistic feasts on large beached marine mammals, and the presence of bird and marsupial bones demonstrates that the ocean was not the only source of sustenance.

Mature trees with large scars indicate the removal of bark to make canoes, although many more trees must have been destroyed by clearing over the last 200 years. Historical records and oral traditions also alert us to the use of bark canoes in the lakes and estuaries, from which men fished with spears and women with hook and line. Fish traps were used in the ocean and in estuaries for catching fish at low tide, using natural or modified configurations of stones, sand banks and depressions.

Other evidence for ancient human occupation along the coast includes a dingo found in the upper layers of the large midden at Nundera Point. The site was occupied from around 2,000 to 300 years ago, and over that time the shell diet changed from the big gastropods such as whelks and turban shells, to the blue mussel — a dietary shift confirmed in many other excavated middens on the South Coast.[7] Human burials can also occur in middens, such as those found in

---

[7] Snelson, W., Sullivan, M. and Preece, N. 'Nundera Point: An experiment in stabilising a foredune shell midden', *Australian Archaeology*, 1986, 23: 25–41.

the Murramarang resort. Rockshelters are relatively uncommon on the coast but two are nearby, at Willinga Lake and the well-known sea cave at North Durras, occupied about 400 years ago.[8]

Figure 5 also shows numerous sites away from the coast, in the tall open forests of the coastal ranges. These sites are mainly scatters of stone artefacts made by Aboriginal people using stone that produced sharp edges when struck to fashion a lethal spear point or barb. Silcrete was a local stone type favoured by Aboriginal people for making tools because it is hard and fine-grained. Some of the silica quarried at Narrawallee from 1919 and sent to Sydney was almost certainly taken from the same sources once used by local Aboriginal people.

Ironically, finding stone artefacts in forests is helped by the very actions that can damage them. They can only be seen when the ground is free of leaf litter, plants and fallen branches, hence most sites are recorded on roads and tracks, and because these tend to occur on ridgelines it seems that most sites are on ridgelines, but it may simply be recording bias. Some forest sites have only one or two artefacts, while others have hundreds. Due to field research by ANU archaeology students during the 1980s and 1990s — which recorded over 2,000 sites in the forests between Batemans Bay and Bawley Point — we can begin to understand how Aboriginal people interacted with the South Coast landscape.[9] While the immediate coastline was a favoured location for living, hunting and gathering, coastal people also utilised the forests for many purposes. They walked along ridgelines, camping on knolls and in saddles or in sandstone overhangs where the walls were sometimes decorated with art such as animal motifs in charcoal or ochre or hand stencils. They hunted forest marsupials and birds, collected plant foods and medicines, honey, plant material for weaving baskets and the like, and gathered wood for making tools.

They also burnt the country to encourage green pick for kangaroos and to make it easier to walk through, although it is hard to find local palaeoenvironmental or archaeological evidence to elaborate on our limited understanding of traditional burning practices. The traditional knowledge required to know where, when and how to obtain these food resources was passed down through the generations, as part of growing up and belonging to 'country'. This knowledge included taking on the responsibility of looking after the land and sea — caring for country.

---

8   Lampert, R. 'An excavation at Durras North, New South Wales', *Archaeology and Physical Anthropology in Oceania*, 1966, 1(2): 83–121.
9   Knight, T. 'The Batemans Bay forests archaeological project', Report to NPWS, 1996.

Yet, life was not devoted solely to harvesting resources; much time was spent in ceremonial activity, often associated with sacred sites or places of great spiritual significance. The archaeological evidence for ceremonial activity can include earth rings (banyan) or stone arrangements, such as the one on Quilty's Mountain. Pigeon House Mountain (Didthol) is known to be spiritually significant and ceremonies probably also took place there, as they did on Mount Kingiman. Many prominent natural features, such as mountains and rivers, are connected by traditional storylines, linked back to the 'Dreamtime', when the world and humans were created. Knowledge of spiritual places, the creation beings that made them and the practices to protect and respect them also constitutes part of traditional knowledge.

These were the circumstances of traditional Aboriginal life prior to the establishment of colonial settlements, the period that Bruce Hamon's book deals with. However, it is important to recognise the ongoing Indigenous contribution to the history of the region over the past 200 years. This includes their role in farming, fishing and the timber industry. In the following chapters, we have added footnotes to Bruce's text associated with this Indigenous connection with the land. While local Aboriginal people no longer practice traditional hunting and gathering and land management, their connection with land and culture remains extremely strong, exercised politically through the *Native Title Act 1993* (Cwlth) and the *Aboriginal Land Rights Act 1983* (NSW).

The Land Rights Act created Local Aboriginal Land Councils who can make application to the NSW Government to claim vacant crown land, which may be granted if not needed for an 'essential public purpose'. Murramarang is within the boundaries of the Batemans Bay Local Aboriginal Land Council who own several parcels of land in the district, including at Kioloa. There are also local Aboriginal families with strong cultural ties to the Murramarang/Kioloa area who are not part of the Land Council system. The local Indigenous community keeps culture alive in many ways — by involvement in heritage work, teaching language and traditional arts and crafts, participating in national park management and educating the wider public about Aboriginal culture.

AUTHOR'S PREFACE

This book tells the story of a small part of the coast of New South Wales: Bawley Point, Murramarang and Kioloa; with some mention of Durras, Pebbly Beach and Termeil. Why this small area? And why me? The two questions are certainly connected. My parents, Les and Alma Hamon, moved to Bawley Point in 1918, when I was less than a year old. I lived there till 1930, and have been back there every year since, so I have known the place for about three-quarters of the time since its settlement.

The idea of writing a history of the area came late. When the Kioloa property, one of the early grants in the area, was given to The Australian National University in 1975 by Joy London, the ANU asked one of their historians, the late H. J. Gibbney, to collect material and prepare a history. Unfortunately, he was not spared to complete the job.

Mrs Lorna Froude and Mrs Dorothy Watts took the project further, but were unable to finish it, so it landed on my plate. My main aim has been to present the history of the area since first European settlement. The pre-settlement background of the district has been covered already in several publications, so is mentioned only briefly here.

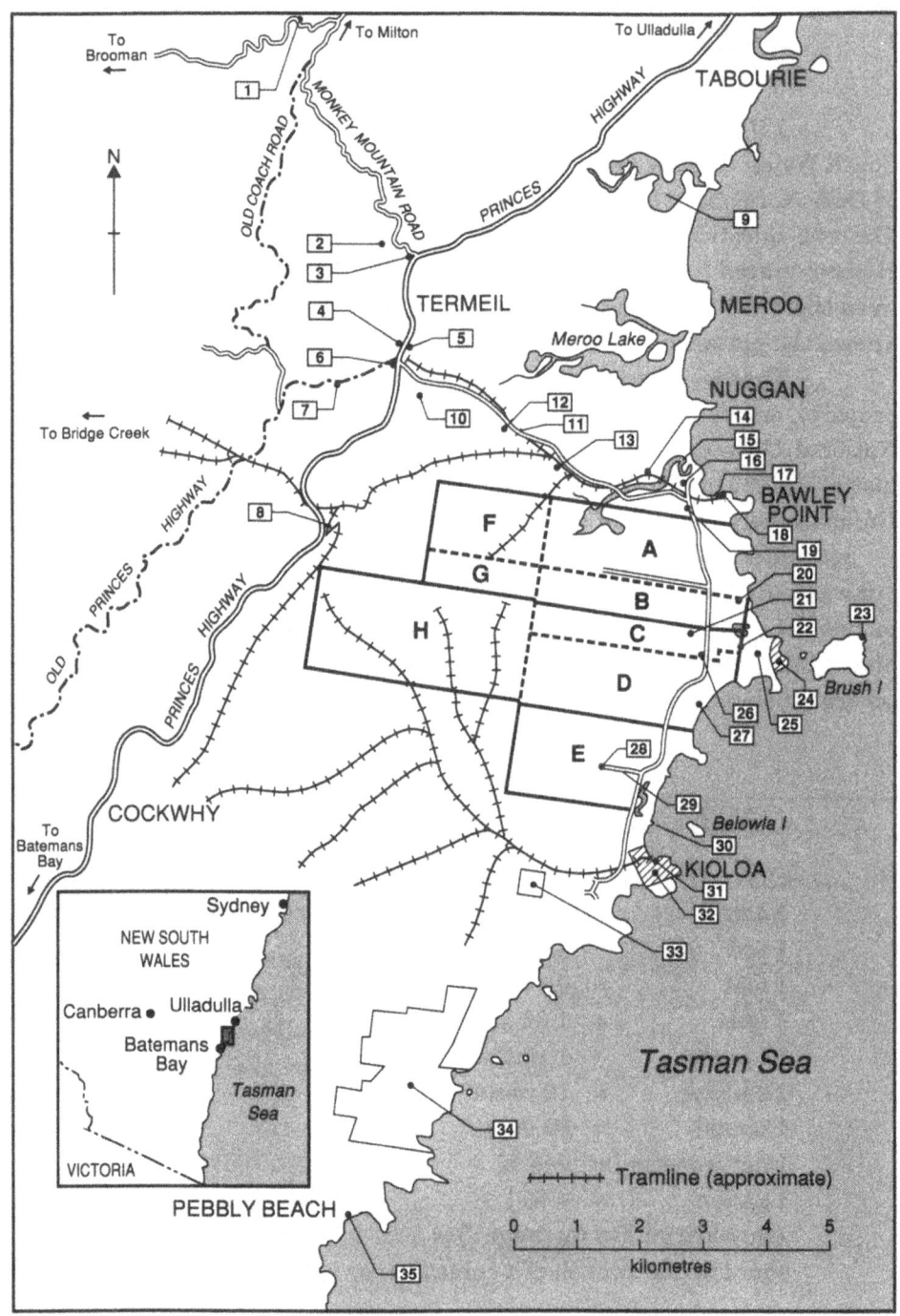

Map 1: Locality map.
Source: Bruce Hamon.

LOCALITY MAP AND NOTES

1. Flat Rock Mill
2. Old Termeil School site (1885–1896)
3. New Termeil School site (1896–1958)
4. Termeil Hotel (~1900); Post Office (~1920s)
5. Termeil Store (~1900); Boarding House (~1910)
6. Present Termeil Post Office/Store/Petrol Station
7. Old Boarding House (approx.)
8. Zig Zag
9. Termeil (Dermal) Lake
10. Bray's sawmill, Termeil
11. 'The Gap' (highest point for the Termeil–Bawley Point tramline)
12. Jackson's sawmill
13. 'The Boiler' (beside the tramline for decades, a convenient landmark)
14. Willinga settlement (~1891–1922)
15. Willinga Lake
16. Bawley Point Guest House (1932–2001)
17. Bawley Point Guest House (1925–1932)
18. Bawley Point sawmill
19. Bawley Point school site (1896–?)
20. Site where 'Woondu' plate and skeleton were found (~1920)
21. Murramarang House
22. Likely site of first settlement, 1829

23. *Northern Firth* wreck on Brush Island
24. Aboriginal midden site; also likely site of early burial ground
25. Wilford's Point (Wilford, a butcher in Milton, used to run cattle here)
26. Murramarang school site (1922–1931)
27. Early Blacksmith Shop site (described by Owen Dent, ANU)
28. Joy London's Home
29. 'The Avenue', Kioloa
30. Butler's Point (site of *Samoa* wreck)
31. Kioloa sawmills (Goodlet and Smith, then McKenzie, earlier pit-sawmill?)
32. Site of Kioloa village, surveyed by Larmer 1845; cancelled 1915
33. Possible site of pit-sawmill; later vegetable garden
34. Early settlement, Durras Mountain. (Block 2–8, Parish of Kioloa)
35. Pebbly Beach sawmill

Early land grants

Stephen	Blocks C, D, H	Area 2,560 acres
Morris	Blocks A, B, F, G	Area 1,960 acres
Carr	Block E	Area 860 acres

These areas are outlined in full lines. Dotted lines show the 1906 subdivision.

 CHAPTER 1
PRE-SETTLEMENT

The Aborigines[1] are believed to have been on the South Coast of New South Wales for at least 20,000 years, judging from dating of carbon found in a cave near Burrill Lake. It is hard to get such a number of years into perspective. A thousand generations? A hundred times the duration of white settlement? We are not used to such scales of time. It is short as geologists measure time, but it is long enough to include the peak of the most recent ice age, when sea levels were lower by up to 100 metres. The shore would have been further east, and Brush Island not an island at all, for much of this time.

Few legacies of the Aborigines remain.[2] Murramarang headland has a large midden which was found by anthropologists from the Australian Museum in the 1920s, and from which many artefacts were collected. At that time, the midden area was bare, with shifting sand dunes that would cover or expose parts of it, so on each visit you could expect to see something new. The present vegetation is recent, and the result of deliberate efforts to 'stabilise' the dunes.[3]

---

1 Today, the term Aborigine is rarely used, having been replaced by 'Aboriginal people' or 'Indigenous people/communities' (A.G. and S.F.).
2 Many legacies of traditional Aboriginal use and occupation of the area still remain. The area has numerous recorded archaeological sites, and one of the best known is the large midden on Murramarang headland (see previous section). Local Aboriginal communities also have oral traditions rich in descriptions of Aboriginal traditional and historical life in the region (A.G. and S.F.).
3 Collection of Aboriginal artefacts was rife across NSW before legislation was brought in to make it illegal without a permit. Many artefacts from Murramarang headland can be found in the Tabourie Museum. The same legislation (*National Parks and Wildlife Act 1974*) enabled declaration of Murramarang Aboriginal Area in 1976, in recognition of its considerable cultural and scientific values. NPWS stopped vehicles driving over the sand dunes, as it was destroying vegetation and causing massive dune blow outs that exposed and damaged the cultural deposits. The area began to revegetate naturally, helped by a NPWS deliberate seeding programme to stabilise the dunes and protect the archaeological sites (A.G. and S.F.).

■ THEY CAME TO MURRAMARANG

The area has an aura of timelessness. But it may have been in use only briefly in the 20,000 years of Aboriginal presence in the area.[4] It is fascinating to speculate on the possible location of earlier middens, now underwater off Brush Island. Was there a 'Murramarang Tribe'? The Aborigines were nomadic, and their social organisation less rigid than might be inferred from our word 'tribe'.[5] For the same reasons, it is very unlikely that there was any aspect of Aboriginal custom that was specific to the small area we are interested in.[6] Aboriginal oral tradition preserved a record of early contact with white people, but the details are not clear. Coomee, a full-blooded Aboriginal woman from this district who died at Ulladulla in 1914, claimed her grandmother remembered 'the first time the white birds [sailing ships] came by'.[7/8]

One family living at Bawley Point is proud of its descent from the local Aborigines. L. W. ('Sonny') Butler's great-grandmother was a full-blood Aborigine. Several generations of Butlers have been professional fishermen in the district. Aborigines now prefer to be referred to as Kooris, but I will keep to the terms used at the time of my story.

---

4   Archaeological excavations in the 1960s showed that initial occupation of Murramarang headland around 12,000 years ago was probably sporadic, with much more intensive occupation following the stabilisation of the sea level around 6,000 years ago (A.G. and S.F.).
5   Turbet, P. *The Aborigines of the Sydney District before 1788*, Kangaroo Press, Sydney, 1989, p. 19.
6   There was a 'Murramarang Tribe', although probably not a tribe, that usually numbered about 500. It was more of a clan or mob, consisting of an extended family, who had responsibilities for looking after specific, well-defined tracts of country together with its sacred sites, storylines, plants, animals, soils, rocks and water. The Murramarang or Mooramorrang group utilised Murramarang, Meroo Lake and Termeil Lake (Wesson, S. *An historical atlas of the Aborigines of eastern Victoria and far south-eastern New South Wales*, Monash Publications in Geography and Environmental Science, No. 53, Monash University, Melbourne, 2000). Many local Aboriginal people today identify themselves as belonging to the 'Murramarang mob'. Between 1832 and 1847, Murramarang was one of several locations where blankets were issued to Aboriginal people and records kept. Aboriginal people came in from across the district to receive blankets and the records give their names and group/location affiliation. Numbers dwindled from 15 to four over this period. Some of the names from blanket issue records can be found at www.ulladulla.info/category/heritage/aboriginal-heritage. The Kialoha group was associated with Kioloa State Forest (now Murramarang National Park) and inland, the country of the Tytdel/Didthol people included Pigeon House Mountain and the coastal ranges. To the south, the Durare/Turras group utilised the Durras area (Wesson, 2000) (A.G. and S.F.).
7   Smith, Jim *Thurawal Traditions about their first European Contacts*, unpublished MS, 1991, p. 8; McAndrew, A. *Memoirs of Mollymook, Milton and Ulladulla*, McAndrew, 1989, p. 36.
8   There are numerous historical references to Coomee-Nulunga, alias Maria/Moriah Billy Boy (her husband's name). Born in 1825, she claimed her grandmother saw Captain Cook sailing past Murramarang Point, which is perfectly feasible, given the dates. Coomee-Nulunga was a well-known individual in the Ulladulla area and features in the reminiscences of a number of Europeans. The couple were sometimes referred to as Queen Maria (or Moriah) and King Billy (Goulding, M. and Waters, K. 2005 *Shoalhaven Local Government Area: Aboriginal Heritage Study NSW*, Aboriginal Historic Research Stage 1 [draft], unpublished report to Department of Environment and Conservation, Queanbeyan; Wesson, 2000). In 1909, a Mr Edmund Milne, who first met Coomee in about 1868 when a boy attending school at Ulladulla, presented her with a gorget (king plate), as the last member of the Murramarang tribe. The gorget states 'Coomee, Last of her Tribe, Murramarang', the only decorations are a series of engraved lines at each point, these lines represent the ceremonial scarring that Milne observed on each of Coomee's shoulders (Goulding and Waters, 2005) (A.G. and S.F.).

1. PRE-SETTLEMENT

Figure 6: Murramarang from Brush Island, c. 1955, before dune stabilisation.
Source: Bruce Hamon.

The first European visitors to this part of the Australian coast were probably Portuguese, more than two centuries before Cook. Ward reproduced 'The Dauphin Map' which he claims 'accurately charts the east coast of Australia and proves conclusively that Portuguese mariners charted it before 1536', but not all historians would agree with this interpretation of the map.[9]

If the 1770 voyage of Captain Cook was not the first visit of Europeans to the area, it was certainly the most important. This, and the work of subsequent early explorers and surveyors, has been covered in many publications,[10] so will be mentioned only briefly here.

I recall learning at Murramarang School in the 1920s that Cook first saw Australian Aborigines on Murramarang Beach. This may be slightly in error; Racecourse Beach seems more likely, since the ship was closer to shore there.[11] The date

---

9   Ward, R. *Australia since the coming of Man*, Lansdowne Press, 1982, pp. 22–4.
10 Cambage, R. H. *Captain Cook's Pigeon House, and Early South Coast Exploration*, Samuel E. Lees, Sydney, 1916, p. 24.
11 Pleaden, R. F. *Coastal Explorers*, Milton/Ulladulla District Historical Society, 1990, pp. 8, 9.

was 23 April 1770.[12] Cook described Brush Island, but did not name it, nor did he name any other features in the vicinity except Pigeon House Mountain. He contemplated a landing in the shelter of Brush Island, but decided against it because of onshore winds.

The first Europeans to travel along the coast did so in tragic circumstances.[13] They were survivors of the wreck of the *Sydney Cove*, which was beached on an island in the Furneaux Group, Bass Strait, in February 1797. Seventeen survivors set out on 15 March from near Point Hicks (now Cape Everard) to walk along the coast to Port Jackson. Only three reached safety, two others having been left behind only the previous day.

Later that same year, George Bass was sent to check on the strait, which now bears his name. He had six men with him, in an open boat less than nine metres long. On the afternoon of 13 December he saw a pole or stump sticking up on Brush Island, which he thought might have been set up by shipwrecked sailors. Due to a 'heavy and fiery sea' he could not investigate at the time, but did land there on his return in February 1798; he found the 'pole' was only a dead tree. He spent the night either on the island or anchored nearby.

The surveyor Thomas Florance was next on the scene, in 1828. He named, or recorded native names for, many of the coastal features. According to Pleaden:

> He did not name either Durras or Kioloa although he called them 'good harbours' which is an exaggeration. Brush Island was called Mit Island, and Crampton's Island, off Tabourie, was noted as Casual Island, neither name being explained. He recorded native names for natural features, many of which have survived in modified form, 'Mherroo', 'Tobowerry', 'Turmeel', 'Bhuril', 'Mherringo' are examples, the first four being easily recognised while the last has now changed to Willinga.[14]

Florance reached Murramarang by 31 May 1828. 'He wrote across the site of the present holdings "very open excellent land".'[15] The headland opposite Brush Island was called 'Aqua Point', evidently for the numerous springs which flow from under the sandhills. He referred to a 'limpid lagoon', presumably the one

---

12   The entry on page 301 of Vol. 1 of *Journals of Captain Cook* (Beaglehole (ed.) 1955) is under the date 'Sunday 22nd.', and the sighting appears to have been in the forenoon. This becomes Monday 23 April according to our date line convention. Dates in the *Journal* can be further confused by Cook's use of 'ship time', by which the 24-hour day begins 12 hours before the day of civil time, and runs from noon to noon (see facing page 1 of the *Journal*). This use of ship time does not affect 'a.m.' times or dates, so is not a factor to be considered here.
13   Pleaden, op. cit., p. 13.
14   ibid., pp. 48, 49.
15   Cambage op. cit., p. 17.

near the middle of Murramarang beach.[16] Cambage claimed it 'remained fresh until 1870, when, during the wet season, the grass-covered sand between it and the ocean was broken through'. At present, the lagoon breaks out to the sea after heavy rain, but also receives sea water during heavy seas. Cambage claimed it was sufficiently fresh for stock to drink during the summer of 1915–16. In December 1829, Robert Hoddle surveyed the land granted to Stephen and Morris at Murramarang.

The next chapter deals with the earliest settlement in the district, at Murramarang, around 1830. To set the scene for this, we might try to conjure up some aspects of conditions at that time, at least as far as they affected the early settlers.

It was only 42 years after the first settlement at Sydney, and 27 years after the crucial first crossing of the Blue Mountains. The total white population in the colony was only around 40,000, more than half of whom were convicts or ex-convicts. For the most part, these people had come from town backgrounds in England or Ireland, and so had few of the practical skills needed in a frontier society. And by virtue of their having been forced to come to Australia, most of them had little incentive to work.

There were no roads and practically no settlement south of the Shoalhaven River. The Milton district had only one settler; the next to the south would have been at Batemans Bay and then at Broulee. Inland there were a few settlers at Braidwood, but no proper roads. Direct routes to the coast from Braidwood would have been only bridle tracks: steep, hazardous and ill-defined. The Clyde Mountain road did not come till 1856. The village of Braidwood was not surveyed till 1839. Access to Braidwood from Sydney was via Mittagong and Goulburn, but the travel time with bullock wagons was six weeks, if all went well, and up to three months in times of drought or floods.[17] There was no vehicle route into Murramarang.

None of the personal amenities of life we take for granted were available. No regular communication or transport system existed. There were no petroleum products, so lighting at night would have been by home-made candle or slush lamps (crude wicks burning animal fat). Even the humble nail, which we would think indispensable for building, was not available in quantity till around 1850; earlier each nail was made by hand by the local blacksmith. Food was limited to what could be shot or caught, or would keep for months.

---

16 This lagoon is known as Swan Lagoon and is partly within Murramarang Aboriginal Area, the rest being on private land. A number of Aboriginal campsites, consisting of stone artefacts, occur around the edges of the lagoon. In the early 1970s it was recorded as a place of spiritual significance to Aboriginal people, with ancestral links to the surrounding area, such as Durras Mountain and Murramarang headland (A.G. and S.F.).
17 Ellis, N. *Braidwood, Dear Braidwood*, N. N. & N. M. Ellis, 1989, p. 165.

CHAPTER 2
SETTLEMENT AT MURRAMARANG

The first two settlers at Murramarang were Sydney Stephen and William Turney Morris.[1,2] I am still amazed at the speed with which they selected and occupied their blocks. Land fever, indeed! Both arrived in the colony in 1828, a scant 40 years after the first settlement. Yet before the end of that year, both had selected blocks at Murramarang, and Stephen at least sent men and stock to start work on his block in January 1829.

Stephen was a member of a noted legal family, and his father, Mr Justice Stephen, and younger brother, Alfred Stephen, were already in the colony. Sydney Stephen and his wife and four children arrived in the *Albion* in January 1828. According to a sworn statement by Stephen dated 10 November 1837: 'The obtaining of land formed part of the inducement for my emigrating to this Colony.'[3]

---

1   Much of the information on Stephen, Morris and Carr came from a 10-page summary of the area's history, which unfortunately has no title, date or author's name. It was almost certainly prepared by the late H. J. Gibbney. In places, I have borrowed the exact wording from this document. I have also had access to copies of many of Gibbney's notes. See also under 'Stephen' on Archives Office of NSW Reel 1184, and *Nulladolla*, Milton/Ulladulla and District Historical Society, 1988, p. 9.
2   William Morris was appointed (or volunteered) to distribute annual rations of blankets to Aboriginal people in the neighbourhood and take an annual census on behalf of the Aboriginal Protectorate. Morris' blanket distribution census of Aboriginal groups, taken at Murramarang from 1832, is a very significant source of information on the Aboriginal population and the impacts of early white settlement (A.G. and S.F.).
3   Archives Office of NSW, Reel 1184.

Morris arrived in July 1828 on the *Australia*. He had been farming and grazing stock at Romney Marsh (Kent, England), where his health became affected by 'Marsh Fever'. He emigrated after inheriting, with his brother, 'a considerable fortune'.

Stephen's selection was based on reports of surveyor Florance, who visited the area at the end of May 1828. Stephen inspected the area, but it is not clear if this was in person or through an agent. Morris had applied initially for a different block of land. Before this application could be processed, however, he met Stephen, who unwisely discussed with him a plan to secure more land by applying, in the name of a relative, for a block next to his Murramarang land. Morris, no doubt relying on his farming background, offered to act as technical adviser to Stephen's agent. He inspected the land, but covertly applied in November 1828 for the very block which Stephen had in mind.[4]

Stephen's original grant was 2,560 acres, and Morris' was 1,820 acres. The locations, and subsequent ownership to 1930, are shown in the map (see Map 1 on page xxxii) and Table 1 (see also Chapter 3). Both blocks were rectangular, with the longer dimension at least three times the shorter dimension, and with the shorter dimension parallel to the coast. This was part of government land grant policy, intended to ensure that each grantee should receive a just proportion of good and inferior land.[5]

The letters A to H in the top line of each part of the table refer to the blocks of land outlined on Map 1. The three earliest grants are outlined in full lines on the map; the subdivision along the dashed lines was in 1906.

The procedure for grants of land at this time was that a settler simply asked for a certain area of land in a particular county. There were limits to the area, depending on the financial situation of the settler. If the authorities approved, the land was promised to the settler. At a later date, he would be authorised to occupy the land. Surveying was fitted in when it could be arranged; there were not enough surveyors in those days of rapid expansion. Finally the actual deed of grant would be issued. In Stephen's case, the dates of these various steps were: promise of land, 22 March 1828; authority to take possession, 18 September 1828; actual possession, January 1829; survey (by Hoddle), December 1829; deed of grant issued much later, on 3 February 1837. The area of 2,560 acres (four square miles) appears to have been an upper limit for free grants at the time, though the regulations about grants and sale of land were complex and they changed frequently.[6]

---

4 ibid.
5 Perry, T. M. *Australia's First Frontier*, Melbourne University Press, Parkville, Victoria, 1963, p. 48.
6 Roberts, S. H. *History of Australian Land Settlement 1788–1920*, Macmillan of Australia, South Melbourne, 1968.

2. SETTLEMENT AT MURRAMARANG

Table 1: Landowners, 1829–1930, Bawley Point–Murramarang–Kioloa.

Area:	ABFG	CDH	E
Year			
1828	Morris	Stephen	
1835	Stephen	Stephen	
1838	Carr	Carr	
1842	Carr	Carr	
1854	Yates and Evan Evans I		
1857	Evan Evans I		
1863	John Evans I, Evan Evans II, et al.		
1870	John Evans I		
1901	John Evans I		

Area:	A	B	C	D	EGH	F
Year						
1901	Trustees for John, Evan, David and William Evans					
1906	David Evans	Evan Evans III		John Evans II	William Evans	John Evans II
1910	David Evans	Evan Evans III		John Evans II	William Evans	John Evans II
1916	F. Guy	(Alf Evans)		F. Guy	McKenzie	
1917	F. Guy	(Alf Evans)		F. Guy	McKenzie	
1927	F. Guy	L. Wilson		E. Wyld	W. Walker	
1928	F. Guy	L. Wilson	W. Orr	E. Wyld	W. Walker	
1929	F. Guy	L. Wilson	W. Orr	E. Wyld	E. London	

Morris also moved quickly. He was promised the land on 10 October 1828, and possession was authorised on 13 January 1829. But he sold to Stephen around 1835, before the issue of the deed of grant for either block, so officially Stephen appears as first owner of the land previously occupied for some years by Morris.

Morris' selection of land which Stephen wanted was a poor start to their relationship, and they quarrelled vigorously. Morris appears to have lived on his property in a large bark hut, from which he and his men cultivated about six acres; they also ran cattle. Stephen called his property Mt Edgecombe, and soon had a neat cottage on it. It is unlikely that he lived there, but there is some evidence that he and his family visited. This cottage was probably on Murramarang headland, south of the lagoon, rather than near the present Murramarang House. The location of Morris' hut is unknown.

The two quarrelled about the possession and use of Brush Island. Morris was given permission to use the island for drying fish. With vague ideas of eventual hunting, he liberated a solitary deer on the island. The deer appeared later among Stephen's cattle; perhaps it swam ashore. Stephen also thought of hunting, and liberated six pairs of rabbits on the island, where he said 'they would be safe from predators, and the crops would be safe from them'. It is not clear whether this was self interest, or far-sightedness. Morris was outraged; he threatened an action for trespass, and ordered Stephen's overseer Garrad to remove the rabbits. Stephen complained to the Colonial Secretary, who decided neither had any property right to the island. Meanwhile, the rabbits thrived, and were mentioned a few years later by Holman:

> Twelve miles from the creek brought us to Mr. Morris' farm, at Mooramoorang. About half a mile from this part of the coast, there is a small island, where some rabbits had been placed, and with which it is now completely over-run. The only conveyance thither was a slight native canoe, made out of a single piece of bark; in which Mr. Galbraith ventured over and had some excellent sport. He observed many skeletons of rabbits, which he supposed had been seized by birds of prey.[7]

The rabbits are mentioned again in 1870 by a reporter for *Town and Country Journal* (see Chapter 3), who stated only that 'the island abounds in rabbits'. Their eventual fate is unknown, and there is no evidence they denuded the island. They have not been present in living memory.

I was brought up to believe Murramarang had been a 'convict settlement', and there are legends about whipping posts and harsh punishments. Mrs Isabel Vider (née Walker) recalls finding a leg iron with ball between Murramarang and Kioloa in the 1920s. Her sister, Mrs Lily Veitch, mentioned being shown a man-trap, and the ruins of what was claimed to have been a gallows on Murramarang headland. I recall being shown a suspiciously isolated post alleged to have been a whipping post.

It is not true that Murramarang was a convict settlement in the same sense that Norfolk Island was, but convicts were assigned to the landholders Stephen and Morris to help them work their land. It was the responsibility of the landholders to feed and clothe the assigned convict servants, and no detachment of troops was provided to keep order. The landholders were forbidden to punish the assigned

---

7   Holman, J. *A Voyage round the World, including travels in Africa, Asia, Australasia, America, etc, …*, Vol. IV, Smith, Elder and Co., London, 1835, p. 460.

convicts unless they were taken before a magistrate, but it was impossible to enforce this in such remote areas. The practice of assigning convicts led to many abuses, and was discontinued in 1839.

In 1837, Sydney Stephen had 18 assigned convicts in the 'District' of St Vincent, of whom two held Tickets of Leave.[8] Presumably all of these convicts were at Murramarang. He also had four assigned convicts at Sydney. Morris had moved from the district by this time; he is shown as having seven convicts at Batemans Bay and one in Illawarra. Four of Stephen's convicts stayed in the district. They were William Carr, Peter Mcguire, Abraham Whittick and Daniel Pierman (Pearman).[9]

The first overseer at Murramarang was Robert Garrad.[10] He had been transported for stealing, and had arrived in Sydney on 29 September 1811. After becoming a free man, he married in October 1826, and worked as assistant overseer for W. C. Wentworth at Camden. Soon after this, he and his family moved to Murramarang as overseer for Stephen. His time there seems to have been short, as he was farming a property in Milton as early as 1830, though the property was not officially granted to him until 1838. The Garrad family remained in the Milton district, where many descendants still live. The Garrad's second child, Elizabeth Jane, born 1830, has been claimed to be the first white child born in the Ulladulla district.

There was no road access to Murramarang at the time of settlement, so the people, gear and stock must have come by sea and been unloaded directly onto a beach, either at Murramarang, Kioloa or Bull Pup.

As elsewhere, trouble between the Aborigines and the settlers soon developed. In 1830, several letters were sent to the Colonial Secretary by Morris and others, including Flanagan at Moruya, complaining that their cattle were being speared, and asking what steps could be taken to punish the offenders. Morris asked permission to 'shoot such of the Blacks as are known to be ringleaders'.[11]

In November 1830, the Executive Council decided to send a military party to investigate. In January 1831, Lt J. Macalister reported to the Colonial Secretary on his visit to the area. He found that the coastal tribes were on good terms with the settlers; it was Aborigines from a mountain tribe who had caused the trouble. The reason was trivial: unlike the coastal blacks, those from the mountains had not been issued with blankets, and felt aggrieved. Governor Darling

---

8   Butlin, N. G., Crowell, C. W. and Suthern, K. L. *General Return of Convicts in New South Wales, 1837*, Sydney, Australian Bibliographic and Genealogical Records, with the Society of Australian Genealogists, 1987.
9   Dunn, Cathy, personal communication.
10 *Nulladolla* 1988, pp. 10–1.
11 Organ, M. *A Documentary History of the Illawarra and South Coast Aborigines 1770–1850*, Wollongong University, Aboriginal Education Unit, 1990, pp. 164–71.

requested that blankets be issued immediately. Presumably the blankets were issued, but this was not the end of the problem. A milking cow was speared at Murramarang on 10 December 1832. A week later, Joseph Berryman, Stephen's overseer (who had replaced Garrad), was told by one of the blacks that three missing beasts had been speared, and a fourth — a valuable working bullock — had also been speared. The working bullock was found and the spear removed.

The next day (18 December 1832), four blacks were killed by musket balls. Two were old, and were man and wife. A third was a younger man, and the fourth was a pregnant woman. There appear to be only two accounts of the killings — one by Hugh Thompson, a contractor for Stephen, and the other by Berryman. Thompson claimed he saw Berryman and his party fire at two blacks who were running from a hut. One fell, but got up and ran again. Thompson was not sure if the black man who fell was wounded. The two blacks ran to a headland where they leapt into the sea and swam to 'an island a little distance from the main land'. Berryman's party fired at them in the water, but Thompson did not know if they were wounded. He only heard the firing; he did not see the blacks take to the water, or the firing at them in the water. Thompson said he asked Berryman if he had been shooting the blacks, and Berryman replied 'yes'. Berryman resented Thompson's interference.

Thompson visited the black's camp on Morris' property, 'where he saw three blacks … all lying dead from Musket ball wounds and the bodies not cold'. Later, some distance from the camp, he was shown the body of the pregnant woman, who had also 'been killed with Musket balls'. Thompson reported to Captain Allman, the resident magistrate at Wollongong. On 29 December, Allman went to Murramarang, obtained a statement from Berryman, then arrested him and took him back to Wollongong gaol.

Berryman admitted going with others to the blacks' camp. He said two spears were thrown, and that one would have struck him if it had not been deflected by a tree. He admitted firing his musket to frighten the blacks. His men also fired. He reloaded, and his musket discharged by accident, but he did not know if this firing caused any injury. The blacks fled. He found a bundle of spears, which he broke. He and his men went home, where they found Jackey Lowder (a black who had great authority in the tribe) in the 'Government Men's Hut'. He asked Jackey to follow him to the house, but a little later, after hearing a shot, found Lowder running over the hill towards the beach. His men said the shot had been fired to 'bring Lowder back'. He sent two men to the blacks' camp to check a report that two men and one woman were found dead there. His men informed him that they buried the three bodies.

Berryman said he had heard that some of Morris' cattle had been destroyed, and that 'he [Morris] a Magistrate had gone out with his men after the Blacks & had fired upon them'. (In other accounts, Morris was described as a Justice of the Peace, rather than a magistrate.) In transmitting the two statements to the Colonial Secretary, Allman stated:

> from what I can learn of Berryman's general character and the terms he always lived on with the Natives, I cannot think that he meditated such consequences as unfortunately happened, on going to the Blacks' Camp. I am of opinion that when the Blacks threw their spears at him he got alarmed and with a view to intimidating them and protecting himself, fired, the other men being at a distance, magnified the danger and without waiting for any directions from Berryman fired instantly; unfortunately with too much effect.

Berryman was held at Wollongong for some time while officialdom tried to decide what action to take. In late April 1833, Berryman was transferred to Penrith. He appears to have escaped trial. In a letter to the Governor dated 19 March 1833, the Attorney General stated: 'I have been informed by Mr Sydney Stephen that Thompson is somewhat deranged, and that therefore his evidence is not to be relied on.'

We leave this sorry tale here. It seems certain that four Aborigines were shot and killed at Murramarang in December 1832, but the circumstances remain unclear. Berryman, who had much to lose, did not try to deny the deaths. There is no hint in the papers I have seen that the killings were officially sanctioned, as might be implied from the statement 'Official permission granted to shoot six' on page 9 of *Nulladolla* (1988). If permission had been granted, it is hard to see why the Wollongong magistrate acted as he did.[12]

The letters concerning this incident give some interesting glimpses into who were at Murramarang in 1832, and what they were doing. Thompson was described as 'under a certain contract for Cultivating Tobacco', and in December 1832 had been there for five months. There was a carpenter, Joseph Harris, a free man. Morris had a dairyman and an overseer, Mr Fletcher. Besides the cattle, which were the source of most of the trouble, pigs were also mentioned.

Names of some people are given: Thomas Sparks, Abrm Widdick and Richd Nipatich were assigned servants to S. Stephen; Michl Goode is mentioned as a ticket-of-leave man; James Roach and John McQuick are named. (The 1837 Muster includes Michael Good, Thomas Sparks, and Abraham Whittick.)[13] Three men appear only with expressive nicknames: 'Grinning Jack' the

---

12 In *Masters and Convicts: Murramarang and Ulladulla*, local historian Cathy Dunn (2006) also states that the references to sanctioned killings in both editions of *Nulladolla* are incorrect (A.G. and S.F.).
13 Butlin et al., op. cit.

milkman, 'Stockkeeper Jack', and 'Cabbage Tree Tom'. The first two of these are described as assigned servants to Stephen, and were in an alleged firing party. The use of nicknames suggests they might have been Aborigines, but if so they would hardly be in a firing party against their own kin, nor would the term 'assigned servant' seem appropriate. It is more likely that they were Europeans. Ward points out that in country areas, 'most working men were known, to mates and masters alike, only by nicknames'.[14]

The blacks' camp was on Morris' property at the time of the alleged killings, but was later on Stephen's. The island to which some of the Aborigines swam is either the bare rock island in the channel between Brush Island and the mainland, or Brush Island itself.

A house is mentioned, but it seems to have been nearer the coast than the present Murramarang House. The house mentioned was near the 'Government Men's Hut' (convict quarters), which is described as being about a quarter mile from the beach, whereas Murramarang House is more like three-quarters of a mile from the beach. These distances, and the description of the Aborigines swimming to the bare rock island, suggest the site of the earliest settlement was probably Murramarang headland, rather than near the present Murramarang House. This is supported by some studies done by Mr Jack Nicholson (Tabourie Museum) in the 1960s, who found fireplaces made of convict bricks on the headland south of the lagoon, also broken pottery (from 1825–1835?) and a soldier's button of the 20th regiment.[15]

Stephen's plans for the settlement were not clear. He did not appear to have considered having a village surveyed, as Carr did at Kioloa some years later. The following extract from a letter from Stephen to the Colonial Secretary dated 5 December 1829 gives some hint that he might have been already disenchanted, at least with the site of first settlement:

> Fearing that he [Morris] should seek further to annoy me, I beg His Excellency's permission to rent this Government reserve at Mooramarang. It will contain from 50 to 70 acres I conceive, of which three-fourths is between my land and the sea. Should it belong to another, it would occasion me to put up 200 rod of fencing otherwise unnecessary; and this I am now anxious to prevent as there is no chance of my settlement being formed there; there being no Boat Harbour within three miles, and no vacant land for a common within a mile. Besides which there is a narrow strip of land of only two acres which could have fresh water, and there no house could be built as the sea is just fifty yards from the lagoon.

---

14   Ward, R. *The Australian Legend*, second edition, Oxford University Press, Oxford, 1966, p. 78.
15   Jack Nicholson interviewed by Mrs D. Watts, 1992.

In fact the nearest Boat Harbour except in very fine weather is at Nulladolla where I wish to erect a store to receive supplies from my farm, and at which place I would request His Excellency's permission to have another allotment.

The 'Government Reserve' appears to be the land to the east of blocks B, C, D (see Map 1), and is mostly the area called 'Wilfords Point' in later years. This land is about 100 acres if beaches and midden areas are excluded. A possible interpretation of the quoted paragraphs is that the area studied by Nicholson had been the first area settled, but had proved unsatisfactory within the first year.

One other site which might have been occupied at about this time was near the middle of Racecourse Beach, and only about 125 metres in from the shore. This site had apparently been covered by sand for many years, but had been exposed again in the 1970s. My information about it is from a short report by Dr Owen Dent, ANU.[16] The primary activity on the site appears to have been blacksmithing, as evidenced by 'the prevalence of iron fragments, hand wrought iron objects, brick, slag, fused sand, ash and charcoal'. A gun flint, clay pipe fragments, a lock tumbler, pieces of porcelain and pottery, and bone buttons were also found, and suggest a 'date of occupation in the nineteenth century'. The absence of any local tradition about the site suggests an early date. We can only speculate about the origins of such a curious site. Some of the objects found at the site have been preserved; these, with Dent's photographs and description, are likely to be the only record, as the site was bulldozed as part of the dune reclamation programme.

Morris sold to Stephen around 1835, and moved south to Moruya. Stephen then began to spend money on the properties, and on the basis of the resulting improvements he applied in 1837 for a second grant of land at Currumbene Creek near Jervis Bay. When this looked secure, he began to lose interest in Murramarang, and in May 1838 he sold both blocks (Murramarang and Willinga) to William Carr, solicitor, of the firm Carr, Rogers and Owen, of Darlinghurst.

A condition of the sale contract was that Stephen would try to arrange transfer of his assigned convicts to Carr. Carr took possession of the property and the convicts, presumably anticipating the official transfer of the convicts. But Stephen claimed that Carr had seized some personal property belonging to his son James Stephen. He then claimed that the convicts should not have been included in the deal, and ordered his overseer to remove the convicts to the new block at Jervis Bay. Carr promptly sued Stephen for damages arising from the sudden removal of his labour force. This case reached the Supreme Court in March 1839, but was settled out of court.

---

16   Dent, O. *Notes on a Site of early European Settlement at Murramarang*, unpublished MS, Department of Sociology, Faculty of Arts, ANU, Canberra, 1978, p. 10, plus 25 plates.

Stephen moved to Hobart, where he again got into legal difficulties and was forbidden to practise in any of the courts of the colony. This prohibition was reversed four years later. In 1850 he moved to New Zealand, where yet again he clashed with his legal colleagues, and was even challenged to a duel. He died at Auckland in 1858. His biography states: 'Stephen had his good qualities. He was accessible, frank and genial; thoroughly independent and abounding in generosity to the poor.'[17]

The present Murramarang House is thought to have been built around 1840, but I have seen no clear evidence of date.[18] Hetty Ingold (née Garrad) stated that Robert Garrad had been 'in charge of builders of Murramarang House', and that they quarried their own stone on the property.[19] This would date at least the start of building as before 1832, as Berryman had replaced Garrad as Stephen's overseer before the end of 1832.

The 1841 census shows one house of 'stone or brick' at Murramarang, and no wooden houses.[20] There were 23 people (19 male and four female) on the property. Their classifications are interesting (see Table 2).

Table 2: Occupation and civil status of residents of Murramarang (1841 Census).

Occupation		
Landed proprietors, merchants, bankers, and professional persons		1
Shopkeepers and other retail dealers		1
Mechanics and artificers		1
Gardeners, stockmen and persons employed in agriculture		11
Domestic servants		1
All others		8
Civil Condition	(M)	(F)
Born in the colony	2	-
Arrived free	5	4
Other free persons	2	-
Holding tickets of leave	3	-
In private assignment	7	-

---

17 Scholefield (ed.) *Dictionary of New Zealand Biography*, p. 328.
18 Archaeological excavations were conducted at Murramarang House when the footings were being replaced. Aboriginal sites, consisting of stone artefacts, were found during the excavations (A.G. and S.F.).
19 Brief file note in records of Milton/Ulladulla and District Historical Society (reference M135).
20 *Nulladolla*, Milton/Ulladulla Historical Society, first edition, 1972, p. 20.

Papers prepared in 1837 in support of Stephen's application for an additional grant of land give some interesting details of what Murramarang was like at that time, about eight years after its first settlement.[21] The Schedule of Improvements mentions a 'cottage residence' worth £400, and an overseer's house worth £100; a brick barn 70 x 40 feet, worth £380, a slabbed barn 35 x 25 feet, and a stone dairy 36 x 24 feet. There were also a blacksmith's shop, carpenter's shop, store, stable, eight men's huts (some containing two rooms), six piggeries, three stockyards, calf pens, milking sheds, milk house, fowl house, 1,200 rods of four-rail fencing, and 134 acres of land 'fallen, stumped, cleared and in cultivation', with an additional 38 acres fallen and cleared. The garden was of four acres, well stocked and planted with fruit trees. Sixteen miles of road had been cleared from the Boat Harbour (Ulladulla) to the farm. There were 600 cattle and 20 horses, but no sheep.

The above improvements are listed in slightly more detail in a notice of sale of the property, in the *Sydney Gazette* of 20 March 1838. The notice does not mention the name of the property or of its owner, but the location and the area leave no doubt it was Stephen's Murramarang property. In this notice, the 'extensive Rabbit Warren' on Brush Island is mentioned, presumably as an additional inducement to the sport-minded, though of course the island itself was not part of the property. The main building is described as a 'neat and comfortable brick-built Cottage containing seven rooms'. Farm equipment and produce included three large stacks of wheat, 'seventy or eighty thousand (super?) feet of sawed timber', 30,000 bricks, and standing crops of 14 acres of maize and two acres of hops. Twenty assigned servants and three 'mechanics' (blacksmith, cooper and shoemaker) would be transferred with the establishment. The notice also calls the attention of any grazier interested in the property to 'the compact and secure Establishment, which has the benefit of three distinct Cattle Runs, within twelve miles of each other, upon which are erected good Stock-yards'. Where could these be? The property itself (blocks A, B, C, D, F, G, H on Map 1) had a maximum dimension of only about four miles (seven kilometres), so presumably two of the cattle runs were outside its boundaries, but nearer than Ulladulla. Brooman and Durras Mountain (see Chapter 3 and Chapter 5) are possibilities, with the land not officially leased or owned.

The above descriptions show there was a substantial input of capital and effort in the first decade of settlement at Murramarang. Presumably the 'cottage residence' is the present Murramarang House, but even if this is correct we have no indication if the other buildings were near it or on Murramarang headland where the settlement seemed to be when the Aborigines were shot. There is some confusion about buildings in another of the supporting papers for the application

---

21 Archives Office of NSW, Reel 1184.

— the deposition of William Jagon. He stated: 'there was a cottage for Mr Stephen's family, a cottage for the overseer, a stone house besides stone in the overseer's house, a stone dairy.' This suggests three residences instead of two.

Figure 7: Murramarang House.
Source: Margaret Hamon, courtesy of Gail Truter.

Murramarang House appears to have been built to a simple design, which has been little modified over the years. Its front, which faced east, showed three gables, with the front door under the central gable. This door opened into a hall, which gave access to the two main rooms, each 4.6 x 5.4 m (main bedroom and drawing/dining room), one on each side. At its western end the hall opened onto a stone-flagged open courtyard. The two outer gables continued to the west over three rooms on each side. These six rooms were the same size, 3.6 x 3.6 m, and were probably all bedrooms. All the rooms had fireplaces. The walls were about 50 cm thick, and were mainly natural boulders of the local basaltic rock, split where necessary to get a more even wall surface. Bricks were used near windows and doors. There was no damp-proof course. The kitchen and toilets would have been separate from the main building. The present roof is corrugated iron, but would most likely have been wooden shingles in the early years.

Carr decided to expand, and in February 1842 bought the 860-acre Kioloa block (block E, Map 1). He held all three of the original blocks for 12 years, until his death in 1854. We know little of Carr, or of what he did with the land. It is likely that Carr himself never lived there. The property was managed for him by Edward Green, who may have built, or at least finished the building of Murramarang House.

Under Green's management the farm began to produce, but there were considerable difficulties in marketing its output. The main transport available was a fleet of small coastal sailing ships which wandered up and down the coast looking for any cargoes offering. There were no made harbours, and the only natural harbour in our area (Kioloa, or 'Barclay's Harbour' as it is called on early maps)[22], which had been commended by surveyor Florance, soon proved unsatisfactory.

Figure 8: Wall construction, Murramarang House.
Source: Margaret Hamon, courtesy of Gail Truter.

In spite of the poor harbour, Carr arranged for a village to be surveyed at Kioloa by James Larmer in May 1843.[23] The site was on and at the back of O'Hara Head, south and south-west of the present Kioloa boat ramp. Larmer's report

---

22 *Map of the County of St Vincent*, W. Baker, undated, Mitchell Library, Sydney, ZM2 811.32/1843/1. Also Thomas Mitchell's map of 1834, reproduced in Pleaden, op. cit., p. 53.
23 Archives Office of NSW, Maps 3257, 3258, and Larmer's letters, AO Reel 3074.

soon killed any idea of development. He saw the land as 'scrubby, barren and unproductive', and found Kioloa harbour 'unprotected and shallow'. There were huts on the beach, which served as miniature warehouses 'to receive bark and other produce from Murramarang until the arrival of a vessel from Sydney'.

Apart from Larmer's report, there is little written evidence of life at Murramarang in the years, even the decades, following the killing of the Aborigines, and we have to be thankful for any glimpses we can find. One such is in the reminiscences of Ann Rees Jones, who with her husband and young family passed through Murramarang around 1846 on their way from Boro (north of Braidwood) to a farm at Brooman.[24] Their route appears to have been via Nerriga then towards Jervis Bay and south along the coast. They stayed overnight at Murramarang. The part of the reminiscences most relevant to Murramarang is as follows:

> Next day we travelled to Murramarang, a station which belonged to Carr, Rogers and Owen, Solicitors of Sydney. But the manager was Mr Green and his housekeeper, a widow named Taylor who had one little boy. We arrived at this place about 5 p.m. after journeying all day. We were met by Mrs Taylor who said that Mr Green desired her to give us his compliments and that he was very sorry he had to go to Sydney and hoped that we would stay till his return, and that we were to have his room, which we did. Here was a fine selection of books originally belonging to one of the Stephens, who at one time had owned the station but had got into difficulties. We were kindly treated. Fruit was brought to us every morning by the gardener. The second day of our stay we were asked by Mrs Taylor if we would like to take a walk in the garden. It was a good step, she said, but if we cared she would come with us. We did not like to refuse. After leaving the house we went through a gate into a ploughed field. I had my baby with me and their father had to take the two boys by the hand and Mrs Taylor had her baskets. I think I had the heaviest load. So tired was I walking over the rough ground that I wished myself back again at the house. At last we reached the garden, which must have covered acres of ground. The grape vines were all training, hanging over the path, the four sides of the garden, and hanging in rich clusters overhead. We had as much fruit and even more than we could eat. The gardener was gathering grapes into a wheelbarrow, telling us he was about to make wine. Mrs Taylor told us that there were two other young men working in the garden for their rations, one named Rutter, the other Raworth, that we could see the former and not the latter and that if any strangers were there he always hid himself. These young men in time made their way to us saying that they were penniless and would be glad to work for us for their rations. We were at last asked to the gardener's hut. Rutter was there crushing grapes into a tub. I asked the gardener if sugar was used in the making of wine. It was afterwards told us that all the grapes they gathered were made into wine and then into brandy, and that the three, the gardener and the two young men drank all they made.

---

24   Unpublished MS kindly made available by Mr E. R. Baker, Hackett, ACT, great-grandson of Ann Rees Jones.

2. SETTLEMENT AT MURRAMARANG

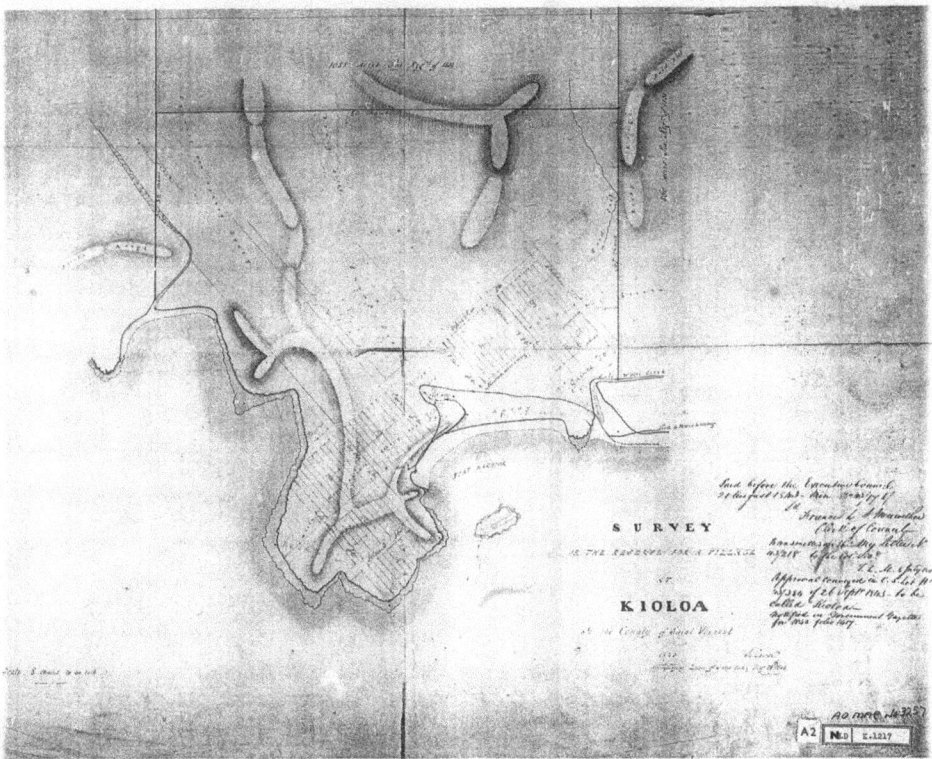

Figure 9: Plan of the Village of Kioloa, 1843.
(Archive Office of NSW, Map No 98). This appears to be a copy of a plan by surveyor James Larmer, dated 28 May 1843 (AO Map 3257). The Village Plan was cancelled 28 July 1915 (AO Map 3258).
Source: Archive Office of NSW.

The reminiscences describe their life and hardships at Brooman. Some of these might be relevant to life at Murramarang. There were many Aborigines in the area, and several comments about their way of life, and food. In particular, the Aborigines ate the burrawang seeds after roasting and soaking them to remove poisons. This was not always successful, and many Aborigines came to the hut at Brooman complaining of illness due to eating this food.[25]

Wattle bark was gathered, chopped up by hand and sent to Sydney, but this was discontinued when a large consignment returned them only two pounds. They also collected and dried wattle gum, and sold it. A large and a small tea chest full of gum brought in nine pounds. The gum would probably have been

---

25 The processing of burrawang seeds and those of other forest species to remove toxins involves placing them in moving water for many days. It is deeply grounded in the traditional ecological knowledge of Aboriginal people and poisoning seems an unlikely explanation for the illness. Disease and the other impacts of colonisation may have hampered the passing on of the knowledge, or the sick Aboriginal people may have come from somewhere else (A.G. and S.F.).

exported as a possible alternative source for 'gum Arabic', which comes from other species of Acacia.[26] Mr Jones visited Murramarang several times, but the visits are not detailed. The 'super' at Murramarang was named as 'Boage' or, in another place, 'Bogie'.

At Brooman they were often short of food. Salt was scarce: the stockman made a 400-mile round trip without being able to get any! One wonders why they did not use sea salt. On leaving Brooman, they called at Murramarang but pushed on to the north without staying overnight. They had a covered 'buggy' or spring cart, drawn by two horses. One was between the shafts and the other 'on an outrigger', which means harnessed on one side of the shaft horse and pulling on a bar protruding sideways from the front of the vehicle. This vehicle had all their meagre possessions, and carried also Mr and Mrs Jones and their three young children. They also had three Aborigines riding 'supply horses'. Presumably the vehicle was larger and stronger than the spring carts that were about in the 1920s. We will discuss their route in more detail in Chapter 6.

---

26 Cribb, A. B. and Cribb, J. W. *Useful Wild Plants in Australia*, Fontana/Collins, Sydney, 1982, p. 269.

CHAPTER 3
THE EVANS ERA

After Carr's death in 1854, the property — 5,340 acres, or 2,163 ha, from Kioloa almost to Bawley Point — was purchased by Yates and Evans for £5,874.[1] The Evans family dominated the local scene till at least 1910.[2] A simplified Evans family tree is given on page 25. It shows only those who owned the land, or who lived and worked in the area. Many other family members would have lived at Murramarang House as children. (See also Table 1, Chapter 2.) I have used I, II, etc., to separate people with the same given names.

We start with John Evans I (1820–1901), and his brother Evan Evans I (1804–1863). They had come separately from Cornwall, England, and were two of nine children of David and Constance Evans. They were farming at Shellharbour when Evan I, in partnership with William Yates, bought Murramarang. Yates withdrew from the partnership in August 1857, being paid £2,803 10s for his half-share. When Evan I died in 1863, the property was left to friends Andrew Thompson and David Warden, brother John Evans I, son Evan Robert Evans II, and son-in-law Wm Hindmarsh. The bequest to the two friends and three relatives appears to have been drawn up without subdividing the land.

Andrew Thompson died in 1867, and three of the legatees (Evan Evans II, Warden and Hindmarsh) sold to the fourth (John Evans I) in September 1870, for £4,500. John I controlled the whole property till he retired in 1900, leaving John II to manage it. But after a disagreement, John II left and took up a property of his own ('Danesbank', near Milton). John I died in 1901, leaving the Murramarang property as a whole to trustees for his four sons Evan III, John II, William, and David. The sons had other properties of their own, so the homestead appears

---

1   Registrar General, Sydney, No. 912, Book 34.
2   Ewin, J. *Meet the Pioneers*, Joanne Ewin, Milton, NSW, 1991, p. 62; Brown, Arthur *The Evans Family History*, Arthur Brown, Epping, NSW, 1987, p. 136.

to have been empty till 1906, when an indenture (legal agreement) was signed, sharing the property out as shown in Map 1 and Table 1. At this time, John Evans II already owned another small block of 40 acres at Bawley Point, north of block A and east of the Bawley–Kioloa road.

In the 1906 indenture, block E (see Map 1) was referred to as 'The Kioloa Block'; block D, which in later years was called 'Bundle', was referred to as 'The Bullock Paddock Block'; and blocks B and C together were referred to as 'The Homestead Block'. Block A is often referred to as 'Willinga'. The block or blocks attached to Murramarang House have traditionally been known simply as 'Murramarang', but the name has wider meanings since the declaration of Murramarang National Park in April 1973.

Robert Ritchie, who married Jane, eldest daughter of Evan Robert Evans I, was at Murramarang in the 1850s, and appears to have been active in running the property. The *Illawarra Mercury*, 1 April 1858, reported:

> Mr Ritchie of Murramarang has gone through with springing heifers, we understand on his way to Dapto. He is the most spirited proprietor in the district in the efforts he has made to improve stock and improve the general mode of farming.

A few months later (9 July 1858) the *Mercury* reported: 'Mr Ritchie has leased 11000 acres of Crown Land between Burrill Lake and Murramarang.'

Between 1910 and 1917, the various separate Evans properties in the area were sold, and the long period of Evans ownership came to an end. But some of the family continued in the area for many years. Perhaps best known in recent years was Neil Evans (1912–1992). Neil grew up in the Milton district. He came to Murramarang briefly in 1928 to shift cattle recently scarred by bush fires. He returned in 1934 to shear sheep for Billy Orr, and stayed on to do some ploughing for him.

Table 3: Simplified Evans family tree.

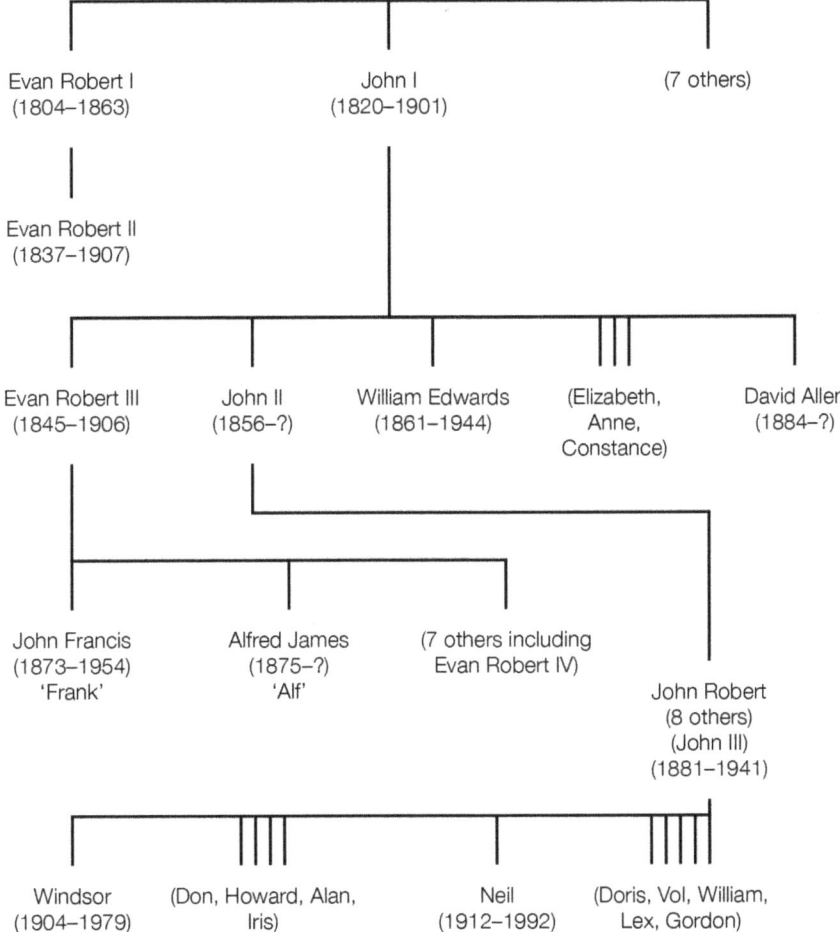

When Orr enlisted at the outbreak of war in 1939, Neil leased Murramarang and farmed it till 1946. Later, after Joy London's uncle (Hum Moore) died in 1966, Neil managed the Kioloa property. He continued there for some time after the property was given to The Australian National University in 1975.

Neil's elder brother Windsor came to the area in 1939. He took over the mail run from Termeil to Kioloa from his cousin Frank after he retired in 1944. Windsor had been born at Willinga, a small settlement on the north side of Willinga Lake.

Frank, Alf and Abe Evans also lived in the district. Frank and Alf were sons of Evan Robert III. Mrs Lily Veitch (née Walker) recalled that when the Walker family stayed at Murramarang House for three months around 1910 waiting for their own house to be built, Alf was running the property, with help from Frank, and both lived there with their wives. Their mother, Mrs Evan Evans, was also living there. Alf had taken over after his father's sudden death in 1906. Mrs Evan Evans was a local midwife.

I am not sure where Abe Evans fits in the family tree. Perhaps he was 'Albert', one of the sons of William Edwards Evans. George Moore recalled that one of the Evanses, probably Abe, lived near the mouth of Butler's Creek in the 1920s, and they boarded some of the mill workers. Mrs Olive Baxter (née Hapgood) said Abe Evans lived in a house behind the Kioloa shop, and grew vegetables.

The Evanses were resourceful and hard-working. Neil, with only primary schooling to start him off, could 'turn his hand to anything', as my mother would have put it. At various times he was a shearer, ploughman, bullocky, builder (including bridges), mail contractor (Milton to Brooman), fencer, log cutter, commercial traveller (machinery representative for Dangar Geddye and Malloch), and property manager. His father was an excellent horseman, and his grandfather bred horses for the coaches between Nowra and Moruya. But in spite of their doggedness and industry, the Evanses left little physical imprint on the landscape. One gets the impression they realised early that Murramarang was not a prime property, so that massive clearing would not have been justified. Neil claimed the land was 'too acid'. A reporter for *Town and Country Journal* (see page 30) was not impressed with it in 1870. Charlie Stephens recalled that Alf Evans was pleased about the sale of the 860-acre Kioloa block to Walker in 1910: 'Murramarang wasn't much of a farm. They [the Evanses] were a bit up against it for money, and I think they were delighted they could sell part of it.'

Figure 10: John Evans II, c. 1900.
Source: The Edith and Joy London Foundation of The Australian National University.

There are no detailed accounts of life at Murramarang from 1854 to the 1880s or 1890s, when sawmilling started. It must have been a hard, lonely life. Distance from markets was a major problem. A trip to Ulladulla, which now takes less than half an hour in any weather, took eight hours or more by dray or wagon, if you could get there at all.

An inventory prepared in 1863, after the death of Evan Evans I, gives some idea of the property at the time. The total number of livestock was 531, of which 108 were 'milkers' and another 74 were 'dry cows'. The contents of house and outbuildings seem spartan:

> **Dining Room.** 1 piano (very much out of order), music stool, sofa, 2 iron easy chairs, 6 horsehair bottom'd chairs, 2 small tables, 1 dining table, sundry chimney ornaments, pair decanters, plated cruet stand, glass [mirror?], 5 pictures, small clock, finder [?], oil cloth.
>
> **Lobby.** 1 large stone water filter, kettle.
>
> **Bedroom No. 1.** Iron bedstead (double), chest [of] drawers, cheval glass, dressing table, 3 chairs (old), night commode, wash stand, toilet set.
>
> **Bedroom No. 2.** 2 iron bedsteads (single), 1 hair mattress, toilet glass, toilet table, wash stand, toilet set.
>
> **Bedroom No. 3.** 1 iron bedstead (single), table, washstand, clothes horse.
>
> **Kitchen.** 4 chairs (old), small table, sofa (old), fender, safe, table, large safe, sundry pots and pans, 1 flour mill.
>
> **Dairy.** 1 barrel churn (about 28 gallons), water tub, empty butter kegs, 120 milk dishes, butter tray.
>
> **Barn.** Threshing machine complete 1 horsepower (in good order), 1 winnowing machine (out of order).
>
> **Outhouses and Premises.** 1 vice, 1 grindstone, 1 large iron boiler (about 30 gallons), 1 chain, 4 bullock chains, 1 large bullock dray (good), one spring cart with outrigger [used for harnessing an extra horse to one side of the cart's usual single horse], 1 whale boat.

Figure 11: Neil Evans and bullock team, c. 1939.
Source: The Edith and Joy London Foundation of The Australian National University.

In the early 1900s, the Evanses had a reputation for making excellent cheese. Mrs Lily Veitch remembered staying at Murramarang around 1910:

> They had about 70 cows, and made cheese in the little shed beside the house, on the south side. Alf [Evans] took the cheeses to Ulladulla to catch the boat. He used a spring cart to transport them — big twelve pound blocks. The road through the swamp oaks was so bad that on one trip the cart's axle broke and Mr Evans and the cheeses landed in the bog. Alf wasn't a very big man, and he had a bad temper — especially to the Walker children — but on the whole he put up with their pranks pretty well.

Mrs N. Guy told me the Guy family had a memory of peacocks at Murramarang. Others recall some old quince and mulberry trees about 200 metres north of Murramarang House.

Initially, the route to Ulladulla was almost certainly across the mouths of Willinga, Meroo, Termeil, Tabourie and Burrill Lakes. This road, really a dray track, appears to have been put in by Stephen before 1837 (see Chapter 2). It was probably continued south over Durras Mountain early in this period. Farming on Durras Mountain had started in the 1860s according to a survey plan of

Portion 3, Parish of Kioloa.³ This plan shows a fenced area around Durras Trig. Station, and a house about 100 metres south of the Trig. Station. James Smart appears to have been the earliest settler; in addition to Portion 3 and the smaller Portion 2, he had Portions 4–8 surveyed by Callaghan in 1879.

There was no settlement at Termeil till around 1880. Brooman was settled earlier. Portion 1, Parish of Albert, was bought by Edward Lord 23 September 1839 for £320, and Portion 2 was initially promised to Samuel Lenox Adair on or before 23 February 1838. It was granted to Lord on 14 December 1840. At this time, the name was spelt 'Burrooman'. There was a road direct from Murramarang to Brooman, as indicated on early parish maps. This would have been the route taken by the Rees Jones family in the 1840s (see Chapter 2).

The following mention of Murramarang comes from a most unlikely source. A German named Hermann Lau spent around four years in the colony, in the period 1854–1859, the last year being at Ulladulla.⁴ On returning to Germany he wrote a book, which was found recently in a library in Hamburg by a German language scholar from Sydney University. Lau had ridden from Ulladulla to Broulee, probably in 1858 or 1859, to catch a boat to Sydney. He stayed overnight at 'a white castle-like building which I recognised as Murrymoreng station'. He was made doubly welcome when it was found he could repair a piano for the lady of the house!⁵ He did not mention names, or discuss the property. On leaving, his way south was over what he called 'Murrymoreng Mountain', but from the context it was probably Durras Mountain. In the bush south of the mountain, and doubtful about the track, he was very surprised and relieved to meet people he knew. They directed him on to MacMillan's, probably at South Durras.

A travelling reporter for the *Town and Country Journal* rode south from Ulladulla through Murramarang in 1870.⁶ He made a good story of the dangers, claiming he 'had been repeatedly cautioned not to cross these creeks [lakes?] alone, as one of them had drowned three persons at three different times, who had been accustomed to cross them for years; another was very deep, and another was full of quicksands'. He crossed Burrill and Tabourie lakes, then 'I got away into the ranges, and, stumbling on a selector's [hut], had to take a bush track to recover the road … I met the dray track on the margin of the Meroo'. This dray track

---

3   Lands Department, ref. no. 957–787. *Plan of 324 acres on the Murramarang Mountain … Applied for as a Conditional Purchase … by John Spurgin.* Survey by Henry Evans, 10 June 1867. The block was apparently sold to James Smart in 1864.
4   Hermann Lau also recorded his observations of the Aboriginal population and their demise in the wake of white settlement: 'became aware of the largest tribe of Aborigines he had yet seen. The Aborigines in general were being rapidly decimated by internecine war, the white man's liquor and various diseases' (Goulding and Waters, 2005) (A.G. and S.F.).
5   Lau, H. *Four Years in Australia* (in German), 1860. Relevant part kindly translated by A. McAndrew.
6   *Town and Country Journal*, 26 November 1870.

would be the 'road' referred to above, and is the most direct reference to its location and use that I have seen. His horse would not cross Meroo Lake, but he found this no problem as the lake was closed at its mouth.

> Another patch of good land appears, and Mr Evans's long white house and outbuildings are seen across the open country … 1000 acres are fenced, and the work is going on, but the grass is not first class, either in quantity or quality. 130 cows enter the bail daily, and the average make-up of butter is 400lb a week.

Figure 12: Windsor Evans felling a tree, 1952.
Source: The Edith and Joy London Foundation of The Australian National University.

The reporter's route south from Murramarang was probably over Durras Mountain, where he found 'a deserted farm' and the presence of some of Mr Evans's cows. He mentioned hearing of caves in the area; we take this up again in Chapter 7.

After visiting Nelligen, the reporter 'swam the mare at the stern of the boat the distance across (quarter of a mile) ... to Batemans Bay', whence he continued south. He mentioned a mailman, who apparently made a regular trip from Ulladulla to Batemans Bay via Murramarang and Durras.

Place names either made a first appearance, or their spelling was stabilised in this period. 'Murramarang' had appeared with many earlier spellings, including Munna Neworag. Its origin is thought to be Aboriginal, with the meaning 'one who is always laughing', but this meaning is from a district near Dubbo.[7/8] 'Kioloa' had appeared on surveyor Larmer's maps as early as 1843,[9] though it was spelt 'Kiola' in the *Ulladulla and Milton Times* during the 1890s, perhaps a deliberate attempt to bring the spelling into line with the pronunciation. This word also is attributed to the Aborigines, with a meaning of 'plenty water' (or 'native bears', according to another source!). 'Bawley Point' appears for the first time in the early 1890s, soon after the mill started. Its origin is uncertain. Clark claims it is from an Aboriginal word meaning 'brown snake',[10] but I think this unlikely, as brown snakes are very uncommon so close to the coast. Alternatives are 'a fishing smack peculiar to Essex and Kentish coasts' (Oxford Dictionary), or a corruption of 'bald' or 'baldy', referring to its bare appearance. It is spelt 'Bally Point' on the Electoral Rolls for 1894–1900. 'Willinga' appears on early maps, and some usages of the word on the maps and in the local paper in the 1890s suggest 'Willinga' might have been regarded as a separate settlement, or the name might have included the present Bawley Point. 'Termeil' was noted by surveyor Florance in 1828, although with a slightly different spelling, so Neil Evans's story of the name having been made up from 'terminus' (of the logging tramline) and 'oatmeal' (grown there as a crop) remains just a good story.

The start of sawmilling in the 1880s and 1890s (see Chapter 4) brought many more people to the area, and must have broken the barriers of loneliness for those living at Murramarang. It would also have provided a useful local market, and more extensive roads. The increased population also saw the beginnings of regular deliveries of stores from Milton or Ulladulla,[11] and so less dependence on irregular shipping for these essentials. Blackburns, general storekeepers in Milton for at least a century from 1870, were the main suppliers of outlying

---

7   Mitchell Library, Sydney, Reel No 2329: *Aboriginal Names*.
8   Murramarang may also mean 'place of beauty' (A.G. and S.F.).
9   Archives Office of NSW, Maps 3257, 3258.
10 Clark, A. (ed.) *500 Names and Places of Shoalhaven*, Shoalhaven Tourist Board, Nowra, NSW, 1990, p. 3.
11 Howard, A. *Ulladulla, before and as I knew it*, A. Howard, Sydney, 1985, p. 19.

areas. Schools, newspapers, mail and even the telephone appeared. The Evans era saw a transition from the isolation of the first settlers in the area to the beginnings of a more modern way of life.

CHAPTER 4
TIMBER!

Timber was always important in the district. The buildings and fences put up by Stephen must have used local timber, but we have no details, except for the brief mention of 'seventy to eighty thousand [super?] feet sawed Timber' when the property was offered for sale in 1838 (see Chapter 2). A substantial timber industry did not start until the first mill at Kioloa, around 1884.

A speculative link with the earlier days might be the name 'Logpaddock' for the headland south of Bawley Point now called 'Juwin'. My father always used the earlier name, often abbreviated to 'Log'. There was no sign of early structures there in the 1920s. Perhaps it was at least a local dumping ground for logs cleared from Stephen's, and more particularly Morris', grants in the first decades of occupation.

Cedar was the earliest timber exploited in the Illawarra district, but it did not extend further south than Ulladulla. I have not heard of any having been cut in the Bawley Point–Kioloa–Termeil area.

The earliest record of a 'mill' in this area is of a hand-powered pit-sawmill owned by Woons (or Woon). Neil Evans claimed it started in 1858, and was on Portion 9, about one kilometre west of Merry Beach. This date seems too early. A map of Kioloa shows land leased to Soulby and Woon in 1882 'for a sawmill';[1] the land was on O'Hara Head, south of the most recent sawmill site.

---

1 Archives Office Map No. 3258.

■ THEY CAME TO MURRAMARANG

In 1883, the *Town and Country Journal* claimed the timber trade was almost the sole industry in the Batemans Bay and Clyde River district, with 13 mills operating and another three being built.² They provided employment for 250–300 families.

The previous issue of the *Journal* mentioned a mill at Redhead (now Bendalong), which was later moved (around 1884) to Kioloa to become the first mill in the district. Their description of the Redhead mill is interesting, both for the mill itself and for the size of township it supported:

> A small township recently sprang up at Redhead, where four and a half years ago the firm of Goodlet and Smith established a sawmill. The mill manager is Wm Pearson, and 30 men are employed. The mill has a 25 horse-power engine, breaking-down frame, 3 circular [saw] benches, and a shingling machine … There were 52 children enrolled at the school.

Goodlet and Smith continued to own and operate the mill, with Pearson as first manager, after its move to Kioloa. It was set up near the present boat ramp, at the south end of Kioloa beach, but is reported to have been slightly further inland than its successor. The millhands lived close to the mill (see Chapter 5).

This first mill ceased operation after a boiler tube burst in 1893. The decision not to repair it at the time was probably influenced by the economic depression, which severely affected the timber industry. After letting the mill lie idle for seven years, Goodlet and Smith 'disposed of all the buildings, timber carriages and other fixings locally', then shipped most of the mill machinery to Sydney.³ Curiously, the ship used for this was named *Willinga*, presumably after the lake or settlement of the same name near Bawley Point.

The firm Goodlet & Smith was established in Sydney in 1856. They dealt in timber, galvanised iron, joinery, mouldings, doors, pottery, and plate, sheet and ornamental glass. Their head office was at 493 George St, Sydney, and they had two substantial buildings in Pyrmont. In addition to the Kioloa mill, they had one at Coolongolook, between Bulahdelah and Taree, and mills in Sydney at Pyrmont and Redfern. John Hay Goodlet, a founder of the firm, had come from Scotland in 1856, via Melbourne, where he met Smith.⁴ In Sydney, Goodlet was very active in public life: builder and founder of the Queen Victoria Hospital Homes at Thirlmere, a director of Australian Providence Society, the Benevolent Society and Sydney Hospital, a founder of NSW YMCA and of Presbyterian Ladies College.

---

2   *Town and Country Journal*, 3 February 1883.
3   *Ulladulla and Milton Times*, 26 May 1900.
4   McClelland, J. *A History of Parramatta's Pioneers*, Pioneer Productions, Sydney, 1985, pp. 65, 67. (Page 67 has a portrait of Goodlet; the original is in the Ashfield Presbyterian Church. Information from Chris Leslie Woods, who wrote this chapter of the book.)

Figure 13: McKenzie's sawmill, Kioloa, probably before the 1916 fire.
Source: Mitchell Library, State Library of NSW.

Although Goodlet and Smith has been taken over, there is still a vestige of the original firm on one of its original sites, as G. and S. Brick and Pavers Supply, Granville.

It was not till 1912 that milling resumed at Kioloa, with a new mill owned by Hepburn McKenzie. It was described at the time as the largest sawmill in the southern hemisphere, and was capable of cutting up to 100,000 super feet of timber each week.[5] It was destroyed by fire around 1916, but rebuilt soon after and operated until the buildings were destroyed by another fire around 1928. Operation in this period was probably not continuous or full-time. The mill closed due to log shortage in 1918, and for unspecified reasons in 1922.[6] The mill was closed at the time of the 1928 fire. The machinery was then moved to Coramba, near Coffs Harbour, where it operated for another 30 years. George Moore, who had been engine driver/fireman at the mill for some years but had left before the fire, was brought back to move the machinery.

Lucy King mentions that a large boiler was purchased for the mill at Kioloa from the old gold mine at Yalwal, near Nowra, and was hauled to Kioloa by two bullock teams.[7] No date is given, but the boiler was probably for McKenzie's mill.

---

5   *Ulladulla and Milton Times*, 17 October 1914.
6   References prepared by mill manager at Kioloa for Robert Moore, dated 30 March 1918 and 5 May 1922.
7   King, L. *The Timber Industry in the Southern Portion of the Shoalhaven Shire*, unpublished MS, Milton/Ulladulla Historical Society, No. M634, p. 6.

In the 1920s, the Kioloa mill employed 72 men: mill hands, log fallers, bullockies, teamsters, blacksmiths, line and truck maintenance men. There were 19 bullock teams and 42 horses, and the mill cut around 5,000 super feet (11.6 cubic metres) of timber a day.[8]

Figure 14: McKenzie's sawmill, Kioloa, c. 1920, with ship moored for loading.
Source: The Edith and Joy London Foundation of The Australian National University.

The mill at Bawley Point was owned initially by Francis Harrington ('Frank') Guy (1863–1931). The Guy family, Francis I, his wife and seven children, emigrated from England in 1841. Their son Francis II (1837–1910) was a pioneer of milling, mining and shipbuilding at Batemans Bay.[9] Francis II had two sons, George Thomas and Francis Harrington Guy (Francis III, known as 'Frank'). It was Francis III who owned the Bawley Point mill and the Willinga property (see Chapter 7). His brother George was also involved in South Coast sawmilling; he is said to have started the mill at Pebbly Beach, and his six children were born at Batemans Bay. One of these (Francis IV, 1885–1947) also lived for a time at Pebbly Beach, where his two children were born.[10]

---

8   *Nulladolla*, Milton/Ulladulla and District Historical Society, 1988, p. 32.
9   Gibbney, H. J. *Eurobodalla: History of the Moruya District*, Library of Australian History, Sydney, 1989, pp. 67, 111, 146, 182.
10 Information on the Guy family kindly supplied by Mrs Natalie Guy, Sydney.

4. TIMBER!

The mill area at Bawley Point was surveyed on 7 October 1891 by Fred Arnheim.[11] The survey plan shows a 'saw mill in course of erection', and 'W B [weatherboard] Cottages in course of Const[ruction]' on 10 blocks each 20 metres wide, west of the mill. The most easterly of these cottages later became my first home. The same plan carries the curious note 'permanent fresh water in rock holes'. I hope this did not lead anyone astray; fresh water does seep into the rock holes, but rarely at a useful rate. This plan has the name written 'Ball-y Point', presumably to stress the pronunciation (see Chapter 3).

From the information in this survey plan, we can assume Bawley Point mill started in late 1891, or perhaps early the following year. It operated with at least one change of ownership until destroyed by fire in April 1922. A report of the fire reads as follows:

> Word was received on Friday last that Bawley Point mill was burnt down, reports the Milton 'Times'. The fire was discovered by Mr. Robt. Allan, son of the manager, Mr. J. Allan, who happened to be in Sydney at the time. When discovered at 3 a.m. the mill was well alight. All hands were quickly on the scene but nothing could be done. The mill was owned by Messrs. A. and E. Ellis Ltd., and was employing 13 hands in the mill, apart from the men engaged in hauling and timbergetting, about 30 in all. Owing to the slackness in the timber industry however, we understand that for some time the mill had been working nothing like its full capacity. It had only resumed operating on Monday last after the Easter holidays.[12]

The Ellises probably took over the mill before 1913, when building of their ship *Douglas Mawson* started (see Chapter 6), but it might have been as late as 1920: the Lands Department Plan referred to above carries the overruled inscription 'Sp Lse 21.1 Febry 2nd A & E Ellis Ltd for "Sawmill" from 1st Sept '20 to 31st Dec '27 Granted Gaz 7 April 22'.

This mill was kept going with difficulty during the 1890s depression. The main building was completely destroyed by fire in March 1894. The coroner found 'that the premises were feloniously and wilfully set on fire by some person or persons unknown'.[13] The loss was estimated to be between £75 and £100. The mill worked only part-time during most of 1895–96. There was a brief closure around May 1896, followed by a few months shutdown after another fire on 30 August 1897.[14] In this case the coroner was not able to say if the fire was accidental, or deliberately lit. Damage was estimated as £400.

---

11 Sketch Plan of Portion S. L. 91.4 Milton, Lands Department, Sydney, Ref. 91.8925.
12 *Nowra Leader*, 6 May 1922.
13 Coroner's Report, kindly provided by A. McAndrew.
14 *Ulladulla and Milton Times*, 4 September 1897. (Gives an account of the inquest.)

Figure 15: Bawley Point sawmill, c. 1915.
Source: National Library, Canberra, ACT.

The two partners in A. & E. Ellis were brothers, Alfred and Edwin. Sid Ellis, son of Alfred, was also in the business in later years. He and his family often came to stay at Bawley Point guest house in the 1920s and early 1930s. The Ellis family were in the timber business for many years, the family name continuing to the present in the Sydney firm Hayman Ellis.

There are traces of iron spikes or ring bolts on the north side of Nuggan headland, but I have not been able to trace when they were used. I believe there was never a mill at Nuggan. Logs may have been loaded there before the Bawley Point mill started. Neil Evans said a single load of sleepers was loaded there for New Zealand during the depression.

The following paragraphs give a brief outline of the operations of cutting and transporting logs, and milling and loading the timber. Practices in the earliest decades may have been different.

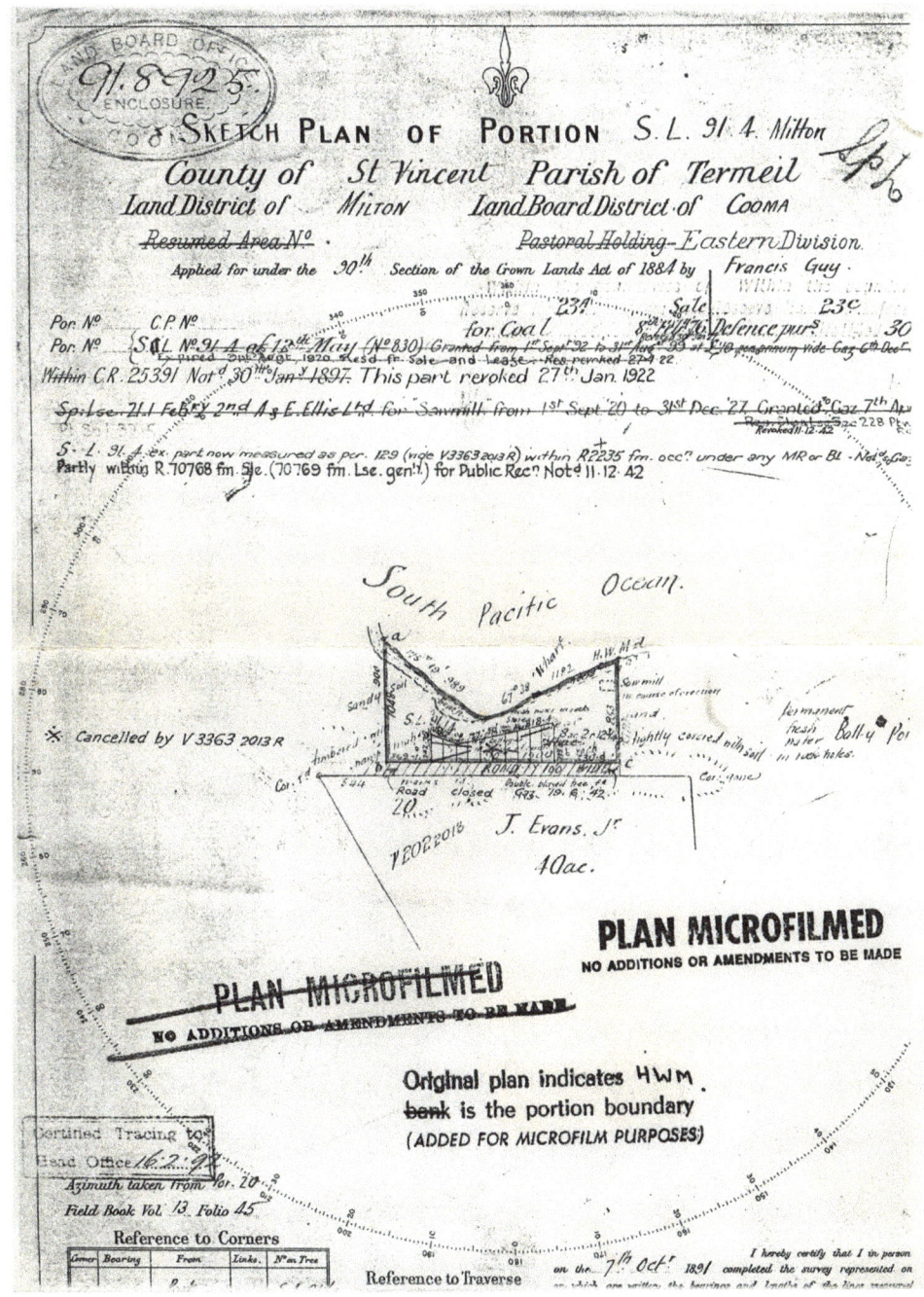

Figure 16: Mill lease at Bawley Point (from Lands Department map 91.8925. Survey by Fred Arnheim, 7 October 1891).
Source: Lands Department, NSW Government.

The tree was felled by axe and sometimes crosscut saw, and trimmed. For the first part of its journey to the mill the log was hauled by a bullock team. In difficult country this might start with the log being pulled along the ground with a chain around one end, a process called 'snigging', but the preferred method was 'punting', in which one end of the log was raised off the ground by using a jinker. This made the work much easier for the bullocks, but they were still slow, so they took the log only to the nearest 'tramline' depot where the log could be mounted on bogies that were pulled along the tramlines by horse teams. The tramlines were specially installed for this job; they extended up to about 20 kilometres from the mill, and had several branches (see Map 1). Their construction involved cuttings, culverts and drainage. The line into Bawley Point crossed Willinga Lake on a specially built bridge 800 metres east of the present road bridge. This line had a branch to Cockwhy, which included a zigzag east of the Princes Highway and north of Stephens Creek to lower the gradients. The tramline rails were 10 x 10 centimetres turpentine or ironbark, spiked to half-round sleepers laid directly in the soil.

Figure 17: Horse team pulling logs on the tramline, Kioloa.
Source: J. Wallace, Milton, NSW.

A horse team consisted of about eight horses in single file. They pulled up to three logs, each on its own pair of bogies. The arrangement of the logs in line rather than stacked meant that pulling up a short incline was a bit easier, as not all the weight would be on the incline at the same time. Brakes, applied by hand-screw to the bogie wheels, were used on down grades. Long, steep inclines remained a problem. The Kioloa tramline descended from a saddle in the Murramarang Range about two kilometres west of the mill, at a spot called 'The Dangerboard'. Here the horses were unhitched and the loaded bogies allowed to run down the incline under gravity. On one sad occasion the unhitching was left a bit late and the bogies overran the team, pulling them off their feet and killing the lot. A similar accident occurred on the Bawley Point line. In this case, the logs making up the load were shorter than usual, so their weight was more concentrated and the brakes were not able to control the speed down an incline. At Bawley Point the horse teams usually made two trips a day from Termeil.

Figure 18: Horse team led by 'old Prince' crossing tramline bridge over Willinga Lake, c. 1914.
Note man sitting on front end of log, and the single telephone line.
Source: J. Wallace, Milton, NSW.

The tramline routes must have changed over the years, but no records have been found. The line from Bawley Point to Termeil appears to have been built around the time the mill opened or very soon after; it was already operating in June 1893.[15] A long tramline was also operating at Kioloa in 1893 (see Chapter 5).

In the early 1920s, Mr Shoebridge, who lived at Termeil, was the teamster on the tramline into Bawley Point. Earlier, around 1915, Henry Browne had the job, and earlier still it was Neil Evans's grandfather, Mr McInnes. The horses were

---

15 ibid., 24 June 1893.

carefully selected for work on the tramlines. They had to have the right 'step', to suit the spacing between the sleepers, but this was not enough. Some horses simply did not suit the job.

Figure 19: Workers and children at Bawley Point sawmill, c. 1915.
Standing, from right: ?, Paul Vider (in waistcoat), Charles Rayner, George Rayner, Billie Page? (with apron, near saw), Johnson (head just above saw). Seated, from right: George Wheatley, Tom Lee, Joe Vider (behind dog), Colin Lee, Lou Vider, Frank Vider.
Source: The Edith and Joy London Foundation of The Australian National University.

At the mill the logs would be stacked to wait their turn. At Kioloa a crane was used for stacking, and the stack could be up to 40 feet high and contain 100 logs. The first step in processing was to cut the long logs into more convenient lengths. This was done at Bawley Point by two men with a cross-cut saw, but Kioloa had the luxury of a steam-powered cross-cut. The milling proper started with the 'breaking down' or 'frame' saw, which had two vertical blades set parallel to one another, about 30 centimetres apart. The log, attached to small bogies by chains or cant-hooks, was moved horizontally through the saw, so it was cut into three flitches, each of which had at least one flat side.

The flitches were cut to final sizes on the bench saw, whose circular blade was about 1.4 metres in diameter. The initial cut on a flitch would be to trim off one irregular edge. This cut was done by eye. Subsequent cuts were made with the timber pushed against a 'fence' set at the required distance from the saw blade. After several passes, a single flitch would be reduced to several pieces of timber of the familiar rectangular section. The sawyer had to cut the sizes wanted at the time, but of course not all wanted sizes could be cut from any one flitch, so he had to make quick decisions to avoid waste.

At Bawley Point four men at a time operated the bench saw, though this was later reduced to three. The sawyer was responsible for setting the fence to control the width of cut, and for guiding the flitch so as to get uniform dimensions. Movement of the flitch was helped by powered rollers at the front and back edges of the bench. The direction and speed of drive to these were controlled by another man (the 'lever man'). The other two would 'tail out': they stood at the back of the bench and received the two pieces cut from the flitch on each pass through the saw. A cut piece would be either sent for stacking, returned for further cutting, or sent via a chute to the waste heap for burning. A sawmill had a manager; other key men were the sawyer, engine driver/fireman and saw sharpener or 'saw doctor'.

There was a second smaller bench saw at Bawley Point mill, used for cutting palings and similar light pieces. A small swinging-blade circular saw called the 'docker' was used when necessary to cut pieces to required lengths. Power came from a steam engine and horizontal wood-fired boiler. At Bawley Point the engine had only a single cylinder, but at Kioloa, at least in the later mill, a two-cylinder compound engine was used. The engines had large flywheels (three metres in diameter at Kioloa). The saws were driven by a system of belts and shafting; idler pulleys were installed so each saw could be stopped without stopping the main engine. The drive to the main shaft from the engine used hemp rope five centimetres in diameter, working in four or six grooves on each pulley. At Bawley Point one single very long loop of rope was used, but at Kioloa there were four separate loops. The Kioloa mill was two storeyed; I think breaking-down and bench saws on the top storey, and docker saw and stacking area below.

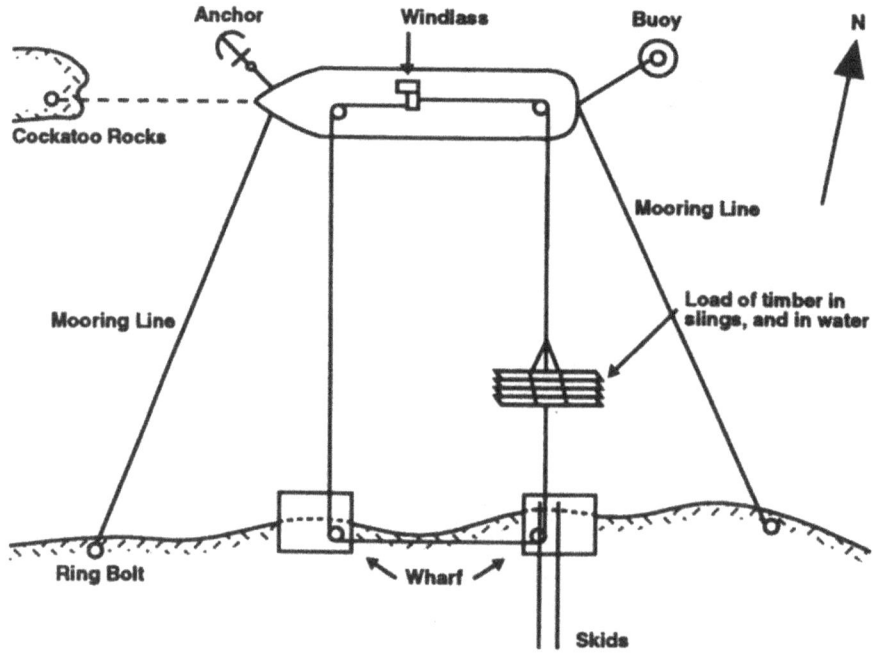

Figure 20: Method of loading timber, Bawley Point.
Source: Bruce Hamon.

Exhaust steam was not condensed for reuse. At Bawley Point, boiler feedwater was obtained from a well at the south-west corner of the beach, where a small steam donkey engine pumped the water to the mill through a galvanised iron pipe. Some reports claim that a condenser was used at Kioloa to get boiler feedwater from sea or well water, but this would have been unusual, and is unlikely.

The sawn timber was stacked on skids in sling-loads, ready for shipping. At Bawley Point the skids were rather too steep, so chocks held in place by chains were used to keep the stacks in place. Eric Simpson recalled that during his time a stack did get away and fell into the sea, and that they had to 'fish it out'. The skids were lubricated with tallow. Timber and waste were moved about the mill site on small trolleys which ran on light steel rails.

The ship had to be moored about 100 metres from the shore. Each stack of timber, held together by two wire slings called 'snotters', was pulled off the skids into the water by the ship's derrick, pulled sideways through the water to the ship's side, then hoisted up and inboard and loaded into the hold or on deck. At Bawley Point, the hand-powered crane on the wharf was not used in the timber-loading process. There was a pitch-covered punt ashore, which could be put into the water by using the crane. This was used to bring bags of chaff ashore for feeding the horses. The crane, often wrongly called the gantry in later years, survived for many decades, and was used by fishermen to launch their boats. The crane, and perhaps the punt also, may have been relics from earlier days, when sailing ships picked up the timber. There are references in 1893 to the use of a punt for loading timber onto the ships at both Kioloa and Durras (see Chapter 5). A punt was used at Kioloa around 1920 for unloading feed. One report says the punt was pulled to the ship by the ship's winch, but pulled back to the shore by a team of bullocks.

In good weather, loading timber into the ships was continued into the night, sometimes even all night, using the ship's lights and oil flares ashore. But sudden changes in the weather put the cat among the pigeons. George Moore recalled:

> We saw on a few occasions near disasters with the ships tied up loading and a wild storm breaking. There was the furious haste of getting the hawsers untied and getting out to sea so the ship would not be blown ashore.

Each mill had its own blacksmith's shop. The one at Bawley Point may have survived the 1922 fire. What a fascinating spot it was for any young nipper! It was the main centre for men to congregate and yarn. I was often bustled off home to protect my innocence, and can remember resenting this. George Moore, a young nipper at Kioloa at about the same time, also remembered the Kioloa smithy:

> There was a large blacksmith's shop at the mill and many essential projects were carried out there. Two which come to mind readily were the fitting of iron tyres to the big bullock wagon wheels also the tightening of them. After the tyre was welded it was too tight to fit on the wheel so a fire was built around it; when it was red hot … about ten men would take hold of it with their pinchers (made on the premises) and force it onto the wheel. Immediately it was in place water was poured on to cool and shrink it. This tightening process was called 'cut and shut'. We also took great delight in watching the big horse shoes being made, the red hot iron coming out of the forge and the proverbial sparks flying everywhere. We also took some delight of the admonishing of the unfortunate striker swinging a fourteen pound hammer and not hitting the exact spot as indicated by the blacksmith.

There was great demand within Australia for timber for some decades after 1860, as a result of the big influx of people to the goldfields. Later, there was an appreciable export market. Much of the timber cut at Kioloa was for export. Peter Scheele recalled that large amounts of flooring and weatherboards were exported to New Zealand, South Africa and England. The timber for export had to be the best quality: no gum veins, heartwood or sapwood. This resulted in great waste of otherwise quite usable timber. In later years, about 40 per cent of the gross volume of a log would be wasted. The best quality timber was described as 'wheelwright timber', though this quaint term had nothing to do with its end use.

Timber of fairly heavy section, suitable for use as girders or for boat building, was also cut in the mills, but very heavy and long pieces, as would be used for the keels of large wooden ships, were usually shaped in the bush using a squaring axe. I was told a keel 30 x 30 centimetres and 18.3 metres long was cut as a single piece at Bawley Point mill.

The timber industry was openly exploitative. You cut in any area until the good logs were gone, then moved the mill somewhere else. Unless extensive tramlines were put in, as at Bawley Point and Kioloa, a mill site might be uneconomical after less than 10 years, as was apparently the case at Bendalong. This situation changed when the road system improved and motor trucks became available to move logs over long distances. George Moore commented on the gloom that descended on Kioloa in the 1920s, when it was realised the time was nearly up.[16] One log-cutter said to George's father, 'I don't know what is going to happen, as we are now cutting the best of the bad logs that are left'.

Some of the other mills in the area will be mentioned briefly. There was a mill at Pebbly Beach, which operated till the late 1920s. It is said to have been started by Frank Guy's brother George, but was being run by George's son Francis Guy IV in the mid 1920s, when Heather Browne worked there looking after his children. The mill was between the present picnic area and the beach, and the timber was loaded onto the ships from the rock platform at the north end of the beach. A tramline with metal rails was used between mill and loading area. Logs were brought down by bullock or horse teams along the steep route of the present road; there was no tramline for incoming logs. At least one accident bringing logs down this incline is reported, resulting in the death of some of the team of horses. This mill is reported to have cut a lot of timber of fairly large cross sections (30–45 centimetres square). These large pieces were cut to final sizes at a mill in Sydney, or exported directly. There was a local settlement, strung out along the shore to the south of the mill, and a school with up to 40 pupils. McAndrew gives the dates for the school as September 1910 to April 1929, but mentions only 17 pupils. These dates are probably close to the dates for opening and closing the mill.[17]

A mill operated at Flat Rock (five kilometres north of Termeil) for many years, but I am not sure when it began. It was operating when the Bawley Point mill burnt down in 1922, and was owned at the time by A. & E. Ellis. Timber cut at

---

16 George Moore, handwritten reminiscences, transcribed by H. J. Gibbney, c. 1975.
17 McAndrew, A. *Tales out of School*, A. McAndrew, Epping, NSW, 1990, p. 134.

Flat Rock was slung under jinkers and hauled to Termeil by bullock or horse teams. At Termeil it was transferred to the tramline bogies and taken to Bawley Point for shipping. My father, who was working at Bawley Point mill at the time of the fire, stayed on there to stack and tally the timber, ready for shipping. This arrangement did not last long. By 1929 ships had stopped calling at Bawley Point, and timber cut at Flat Rock was being taken to Ulladulla by motor truck for shipping. My father worked at the Flat Rock mill for a few years before the mill shut down during the depression. It started again afterwards, but was burnt down in 1949.[18]

There were mills at Brooman, Benandra, Bridge Creek (about eight kilometres west of Termeil) and East Lynne. In later years, and at different times, there were four mills at Termeil. One (Jackson's) was at 'The Gap', about two kilometres east of Termeil, on the Bawley Point road. It closed in 1939. Another (Bray's) was half a kilometre east of the present highway, and south of the Bawley Point road; it began around 1950. Chapman had a mill on or near the old boarding house site, on the old highway south of Termeil, from 1930s to 1950s, and Don Baxter still runs a mill near Monkey Mountain. Charlie Mison had a mill west of Murramarang; it started some decades ago, and closed about 1985. All these mills were smaller than the earlier mills, and employed fewer people.

In more recent years, there has been a tendency towards even smaller mills. 'Spot' mills have only a single bench saw with a circular blade; the initial breaking down being done with a chain saw. 'Swing' saws also used a single circular blade, but in this case the blade and its 10-kilowatt petrol or diesel motor were mounted on wheels, and were moved over the timber being cut. These mills could be operated by two or three men.

The advent of tractors and motor lorries, and the improvement in roads, meant less call for working bullocks or horses. Bullocks were still useful near where the logs were cut, and the Rixons and Drurys still had working bullock teams at Termeil or further west as late as 1973.[19]

Working conditions for mill hands in the larger mills were poor. Much depended on the manager and the mill boss who had power to hire and fire. The mill boss appears to have been a foreman, but that term was not used. Eric Simpson, whose father John David Simpson had taken up a 200-acre selection at Termeil around 1907, got his first job at Bawley Point mill around 1918, when he was 15 years old. At that time they worked 48 hours a week, 7 a.m. to 5 p.m. each week day and four and three-quarter hours on Saturday. There were two breaks during the day, the first which was called 'Joe' was at 9.30, with a longer lunch break

---

18   ibid., p. 138.
19   *Sydney Morning Herald*, 10 May 1973, p. 14.

later. (The name 'Joe' for the morning tea break has always provoked interest, and many individuals have been suggested as the original 'Joe', but its origin might go back a long way. Hammond noted its use on all the goldfields, initially to warn mates that police were coming, but later to attract attention to anything amusing.[20] Since many miners must have drifted into the timber industry, it is easy to imagine they brought 'Joe' with them, and adapted its meaning.)

Most mill workers wore aprons, usually of leather, since a lot of pushing of the heavy pieces of timber was required. Surprisingly, gloves were not always used. The hands became tough, and green timber is not as splintery as dry wood.

The boilers had to be cleaned inside, to remove scale. The boiler at Bawley Point consisted basically of two steel tubes, one inside the other, but with their axes displaced. The fire was in the inner tube, and the water and steam in the space between the tubes. Eric Simpson recalled disliking the cleaning job; there was not much room in the narrowest part of the space between the cylinders, and he was afraid of getting stuck there. Eric told the story of 'a young chap who climbed up to look at the safety valve, which was just about to blow off. He put his finger on it, and it started — and frightened the life out of him!' My own memories of the mill are vague as I was only four years old when it burnt down, but I do recall being afraid of the machinery, which looked immense and threatening to a small child. Not a good start for an engineer.

Wages in the industry were low; a wage book for Brooman mill in 1924 showed an hourly rate of two shillings and a penny,[21] making it £5 ($10) for a 48-hour week. Eric Simpson commented that wages in most mills were lower than this. The toilet facilities at Kioloa were described by George Moore as:

> simple and hygienic. The toilet was built on the edge of the wharf over the water, and anyone sitting there meditating could watch all the fish swimming underneath. The more the toilet was used the more fish.

At Bawley Point the facilities were even simpler: you squatted on the rocks to the east of the sawdust heap, where the next tide would clean the area.

Cutting railway sleepers was an industry separate from sawmilling. The sleeper-getters worked more as individuals, or as loosely organised small groups, and all the work was done by hand at the site where the log was felled. There was great demand for sleepers in the early 1900s, both for use in Australia and for export, and the industry in its original form lasted for around 50 years.

---

20 Hammond, M. J. *Remembered with Pride*, Maruba Press, Lewisham, 1988, p. 41.
21 Shown to me by Jack Wallace, Milton.

The methods were simple, but required skill and lots of hard work. The log was cut with a cross-cut saw into several pieces, each the length of the finished sleepers. Each piece was then split along the grain, using a maul and wedges, to give slightly oversized billets. These were shaped to final size using a broad axe or, in earlier years, an adze. The reason for shaping sleepers by hand, rather than putting them through a sawmill, was due to strength and safety of the final product. Hand-cut sleepers must have the grain running from end to end, whereas milled sleepers could have wandering grain in the timber, leading to warping and even splitting along the grain during service. The ban on sawn sleepers was lifted in later years, probably around 1950, and wooden sleepers are now being replaced by concrete.

The sleepers were moved to the nearest shipping port by any available means — usually bullock teams in the early days. They had to be passed by a government inspector before being bought by an agent. Loading was similar to the loading of sawn timber, but was frequently done directly from a beach, with only rough skids.

Charlie Stephens, at the tender age of 12, had come from Sydney to Kioloa around 1906 to join his father and brother Bill in a sleeper-cutter's camp at Johnson's Creek, two kilometres west of Kioloa.[22] There were 15 to 20 men in the camp, but no women. The men did not stop long. In those days, they didn't have much — a broad axe, a bundle of wedges, a cross-cut saw, their clothes, and perhaps a tent. The ship Charlie remembered coming to pick up sleepers was the old *Queen Bee*. It was apparently a steamer, but underpowered: 'they reckoned they had to stop the engine to blow the whistle!' Loading was from the beach, and the sleeper-cutters had to come in from their camp to help with the loading: Kioloa mill had not been rebuilt at that time, so there were no men about to lend a hand.

Pit props for use in mines were another special-purpose timber product of the district. These were left in the round, another safety requirement. From memory they were around 15–20 centimetres in diameter, so were cut more easily than sleepers.

The following brief notes on the industry in general are based on a recent book published by the Forestry Commission of New South Wales.[23] This interesting and readable account has many photographs and first-hand descriptions of working conditions and techniques. Licences for cutting timber were required as early as 1820, but it was impossible to police the regulations. Some forest reserves were set up by 1871, and the poet Henry Kendall was appointed first

---

22   Charlie Stephens interviewed by H. J. Gibbney, 16 May 1976.
23   Hannah, H. *Forest Giants: Timbergetting in the New South Wales Forests 1800–1950*, Forestry Commission of NSW, Sydney, 1986.

Inspector of Forests in 1881. The Forestry Commission was not set up till 1916, after which date controls over areas to be cut, and size of tree, were introduced. The industry had a reputation for low pay, due to competition from softwoods imported from countries with more efficient milling techniques. Carpenters preferred the imported timbers as they were easier to work. There were almost no safety measures until the 1940s, and no compensation for injuries till around 1930. Missing limbs or fingers were 'a trademark of the industry'. There was little union activity and very few strikes.

We might end by recording the names of those killed in the industry in the Murramarang district; their names are from a much longer list for the whole shire, compiled by Jack Wallace, Milton:

> Pross Andrews (Kioloa, before 1910): A jinker pole fell while slinging a log.
>
> Jack Bennett (Kioloa, 1910): Riding on a dray load of sleepers when dray overturned.
>
> Jack Donovan (Termeil, 1964): Hit by limb while falling logs.
>
> Greg Hughes (Termeil, 1946, age 16): Unloading logs using a wallaby jack.
>
> Fred Tetley (Durras, 1959): Wire rope offsiding for a 'dozer'.

Figure 21: Bawley Point mill site, 1976.
Source: The Edith and Joy London Foundation of The Australian National University.

CHAPTER 5
TURN OF THE CENTURY

The turn of the century was a time of change: roads extended and improved; deliveries from stores in Milton and Ulladulla began; dependence on ships for supplies declined; the ships were changing from sail to steam; schools were established. But the 1890s were depression years, and many families suffered great hardship.

The history of the schools in the area (and in fact in the whole Milton–Ulladulla district) has been given in detail by McAndrew.[1] The difficulties and expense of providing schooling in developing areas led to many different arrangements, which seem quaint by modern standards.[2] Thus we find provisional schools, set up as the result of a petition from local residents, where the petitioners had to provide the school building, guarantee a minimum enrolment of 15 and an effective attendance of at least 10. Such a school could be reclassified as a public school if the enrolment reached 20 and an attendance of 15 was maintained. Some schools were run half time with another school, with only one teacher. The usual arrangement was two days at the first school and three days at the second in a given week, then three days and two days respectively the following week. If there was trouble finding a suitable building, the system provided for house-to-house schooling, as operated at East Lynne from 1884 to 1888. If you could not guarantee a minimum attendance, the system provided for subsidised schools, where the parents provided both the building and the teacher, and the Department provided a subsidy for each student. No official records of subsidised schools were kept, so we do not know how many of these

---

1 McAndrew, A. *Tales out of School*, A McAndrew, Sydney, 1990.
2 ibid., pp. 43, 118.

operated in the area. Flat Rock School, 1940–1942, was one such.[3] If settlement was so sparse that none of the above methods applied, you had to fall back on correspondence.

Kioloa and Termeil schools both began in 1885, and Bawley Point School in 1894. The first Kioloa school building, and its furniture, were moved from Red Head when the mill was moved.[4] This school was probably near the mill, where most of the workers lived. The teacher in 1892 was Arthur Wilson. This school closed in December 1893, after the mill closed. There was no school at Kioloa till milling resumed in 1912, when a schoolhouse was built a short distance south-east of Walker's (presently Joy London's) house at the top of 'The Avenue' (see Chapter 6). Teachers at this school were Beattie, Turner, Stanford, Allen and Walsh. This school operated till the opening of a new school at Murramarang, to serve both Bawley Point and Kioloa, in 1922. Murramarang School (teachers Hayes, Brown, Bullen and Chilstone) closed in 1931,[5] and some years later (around 1936) a third school building was built at Kioloa, north of The Avenue. This building is still standing, but was moved closer to The Avenue after 1975, and converted to an amenities block for the Edith and Joy London Foundation. Teachers at this school were Mr Bone, Mollie Lenehan and finally Mrs Scott, who eventually found the walk from her home near Merry Beach too tiring, so schooling was continued for some time in Mrs Scott's home.

Termeil's first school was built by H. Bevan, a local landholder, and was a 'snug slab building (20 x 14 x 8 feet) with a fireplace'.[6] It was probably on Portion 31, Parish of Termeil, about half a kilometre west of the site of a later school (Portion 97, where Monkey Mountain Road joins Princes Highway). It was used as an evening school in 1886, but this initial enthusiasm did not last. The school building was soon found inadequate and the site inconvenient,[7] so a new school was built on Portion 97 in 1897. This building is still standing, and in use as a private home.

---

3   ibid., pp. 137–8.
4   ibid., p. 110.
5   Murramarang School closed temporarily between August 1929 and May 1931, and during this period Bruce attended Termeil School (See Alex McAndrew, *Tales Out of School*, A. McAndrew, Epping, NSW, 1990, p. 137) (A.G. and S.F.).
6   ibid., p. 119.
7   *Ulladulla and Milton Times*, 1 July 1893.

5. TURN OF THE CENTURY

Figure 22: Kioloa school house being relocated closer to The Avenue.
Source: The Edith and Joy London Foundation of The Australian National University.

The first teacher at Termeil was William Chaseling. Later there were at least two women who deserve special mention. One was Eliza Kellett, who taught there around 1887–89. In later years she corresponded with Mr J. W. Vidler of Falls Creek, who sent extracts of the correspondence to the *Ulladulla and Milton Times*.[8] Eliza often visited Kioloa at weekends, and knew the mill manager, Mr Pearson, 'an old Scotch gentleman', and Mr McMahon, the mill foreman. The schoolmaster was Mr Jamieson, and there were around 100 pupils. She and a friend often visited on board Goodlet and Smith's steamer when she was in on one of her regular fortnightly visits to pick up timber. They fished from the ship, and often caught big snapper. She did not mention Bawley Point or Willinga; perhaps the route to Kioloa did not pass through Bawley Point at that time, as it was a few years before the mill started at Bawley Point.

Eliza taught at several other schools before marrying a Mr Gunter, and retiring from teaching. She lived to within a few weeks of 106 years of age. When well past her century, an interview with her was taped by a relative. I have had the pleasure of listening to part of this, and I was much impressed. It was a

---

8   *Ulladulla and Milton Times*, 21 September 1962.

THEY CAME TO MURRAMARANG

bridge over generations, as I had spent the years 1929 and 1930 as a pupil at Termeil. The second lady deserving special mention is Mrs Will Boag (née Annie McDonald), who retired in 1926 after teaching at Termeil for 35 years.[9]

Bawley Point School started as a Provisional School in September 1894, and continued with some breaks and many changes of status till 1922.[10] It was half-time with Kioloa for two periods, and with the more distant Brooman for two other periods. The mill owner, Mr Guy, provided a four-roomed workman's cottage for use as the school, but expected the parents to pay threepence per week per child as rent. Times were hard, the men were on half pay, so very little was collected. The school was destroyed by fire on 1 August 1897.[11]

The site of this first ill-fated school is not known. A sketch in the State Archives, dated 9 September 1893, shows a proposed school site east of the present easterly limit of settlement on Bawley Point, just north of Cormorant Beach, but there is nothing to indicate this site was actually used.

Figure 23: Termeil School, on Old Schoolhouse Road, off Monkey Mountain Road.
Source: Margaret Hamon.

9   *Nowra Leader*, 9 April 1926.
10 McAndrew op. cit., pp. 127–9.
11 *Ulladulla and Milton Times*, 4 September 1897.

A public school site at Bawley Point had been dedicated in November 1896. This site was Portion 96, Parish of Termeil: a two-acre block on the western side of the road to Kioloa, almost opposite the present shop. A school was on this site around 1910, but it is not clear when it was built. Bill Cullen, who started school there under Mr Stanford around 1916, remembered it as 'a little wooden place ... most likely built of slabs'.[12] Mrs Lily Veitch (née Walker) also remembered 'the little school: a little slab building on the hillside on the left as you go in [from Kioloa]'.[13] And Charlie Stephens referred to it as 'the little school was stuck up in the tea-tree, you could never ever find it. You could hardly see it.'[14] This school also burned down, and pupils then went to a temporary school, a single room in a private house on the north side of Willinga Lake, where the teacher was Mr White. This temporary school must have sufficed till Murramarang School started in 1922. Built on land donated by Lindsay Wilson, Murramarang School operated till December 1931, with a brief closure from August 1929 to May 1931, after which it was moved to near Eden. It was my first school.

In February 1893, the local paper published two articles by 'Mariner', who travelled on horseback from Ulladulla to South Durras.[15] The route 'crossed five lakes ... two were crossed by bridges; and the remaining three were shallow'. Presumably the bridges were over Burrill and Tabourie lakes, and the shallow lakes were Termeil, Meroo and Willinga. Mere mention of the lakes implies that their crossing was regarded as risky.

'Mariner' did not mention Bawley Point, which is curious, as the mill should have been under construction if not actually working. He was not impressed by Kioloa, which he found 'a desert of sand, upon which stood a dozen or more houses, which were by no means imposing in appearance'. The 'desert of sand' seems a strange description, but could fit the area near the mill site, including much of O'Hara Head. Some later photographs show much less than the present level of vegetation, and the soil is sandy.

'Mariner' inspected Kioloa mill, which he said sent between 140,000 and 150,000 super feet of timber each month to Sydney. Some of the logs came nine miles 'on trucks, which are run on rails', so the tramline system must have been established early. A punt was used to take timber out to the schooner *Samoa*. This vessel carried 45,000 to 50,000 super feet of timber.

---

12   Interview with H. J. Gibbney, 4 October 1976.
13   Interview with H. J. Gibbney, 3 October 1976.
14   Interview with H. J. Gibbney, 16 May 1976.
15   *Ulladulla and Milton Times*, 18 and 25 February 1893.

The men at the mill worked ten hours a day, which was considered 'fair', as was their wage of about £2 10s a week. There were 30 or so men employed at or in connection with the mill. The manager was Mr Gibson.

Mariner's route south appears to have been over Durras Mountain, where he found McKay's farm, and commented on the difficulties of marketing its produce 'about twenty-six miles, in a cart, over some of the worst vehicular roads in the colony'. Further south, he found a small village and another sawmill managed by Mr McMillan. This was probably at South Durras. The mill cut the usual timbers used in the building trades, but also had a band saw, used to cut felloes, the curved segments that make up the rim of a dray wheel. As at Kioloa, a punt was used to take the timber out to the ships. A tramline was also mentioned, but here it was between the mill and the loading point on the shore. The ships *Lena Lillian*, a small ketch, and the larger *May Howard* took around 112,000 super feet of timber to Sydney each month. The mill employed around 24 men, who were paid 7–9s a day.

It appears from the comments of 'Mariner' that workers at Kioloa and Durras were paid in the normal way, but those at Bawley Point were not so lucky. Up to the time of the fire at Bawley Point mill (September 1897), the workers operated under the 'truck' system, meaning that goods were supplied to them by the company, in lieu of wages. This unpopular method was abandoned when work resumed in November 1897.[16]

Mining has never played a significant role in the local economy. The hard times of the 1890s forced people to try anything to earn money. Twenty-seven ounces of gold, valued at £108, were obtained by a party of three working for six months on Murramarang Beach in 1896.[17] The following year some prospecting was done there, but with little success. But at Termeil a shaft about 40 feet deep was sunk by Sinclair and party, and some very fair prospects obtained. The 1898 report of the Mines Department said four men had done a little washing for gold from the sand at Murramarang Beach, but it did not pay.

An advertisement in the *Ulladulla and Milton Times*, 4 April 1896, sounded very hopeful: 'We are in receipt of the prospectus of the Great Pacific Beach Gold Mining Company, Murragorang Bay, near Ulladulla … The idea is to work the black sand near Bawley Point by a patent electric gold-saver.' Perhaps the advertisement was intended for 1 April?

---

16   *Ulladulla and Milton Times*, 2 October 1897.
17   Department of Mines, *Annual Report*, 1896, p. 32.

5. TURN OF THE CENTURY

The very fine gold on Murramarang Beach was tackled again when the next depression came round, in the 1930s. Bill Cullen recalled Joe Saunders and Dick Hapgood 'washing for gold on Murramarang beach near the lagoon. They had a hand pump and dug the black sand and washed it over a quicksilver plate [copper plate coated with mercury]. This was the only way they could trap the gold, since it was so fine.'[18]

Belle Vider (née Walker) remembered an old chap at Kioloa, Dick Sampson, who used to do rouseabout work:

> He would disappear at weekends, looking for gold. He had some gold, which he kept in a bottle. Before he died, he told his mates: 'if you can find my pick and shovel four miles due west of Murramarang, that's where I found the gold'. No one ever found the pick and shovel.

The Collinses recalled that shellgrit was mined at Kioloa for a short period by the Kellys, who had a plant at Burrill for converting the shellgrit to lime.[19] Later, during the Depression, a Mr Latta collected shellgrit from Kioloa and took it to Sydney by truck. The Kioloa Parish map shows two mineral leases for 'sea shells': one on Nundera Point and one slightly east of the mill site. Termeil Parish map shows three such leases: two on Brush Island and one on the south of Meroo headland.[20]

The 'Trig Station' on Bawley Point was established in 1892. It is officially known as 'Termeil' station; presumably this name was chosen before Bawley Point was established. The station is part of a trigonometrical survey of the State, which was started in Sydney around 1880. The idea behind the survey is simple: a base line is chosen, and its length measured as accurately as possible. By measuring angles from each end of the baseline to a third point, the position of the third point can be calculated by simple trigonometry. Any two of the three points can then be related to a fourth point, and the process repeated, measuring angles only, until the whole State is covered. The 'points' became the 'trig stations', and served as reference points for subsequent more detailed surveys. The station on Bawley Point was related in the original survey to stations on Pigeon House, Durras Mountain and Warden's Head (Ulladulla). The station is a survey mark in concrete at ground level. Initially there was a cairn of loose rocks and a central wooden pole above the station, but this was destroyed by vandals and replaced by the present concrete block in 1974.

---

18 Interview with H. J. Gibbney, 4 October 1976.
19 McAndrew, A. *Beautiful Burrill*, A. McAndrew, 1993, pp. 82–5.
20 Shellgrit mining would have almost certainly involved taking material from the Aboriginal shell middens at Nunderah Point and elsewhere in the region (A.G. and S.F.).

Postal services in the district started in 1889, as a result of a petition from residents at Termeil, Kioloa, Murramarang (Thomas Gould, farmer, and Arthur Gumley, farm labourer), and Durras Mountain (E. Smart, farmer).[21] Neither Bawley Point nor Willinga was mentioned; presumably these places were not yet settled.

Arthur Baxter was the first postmaster at Termeil, starting duty on 1 September 1889. The office was at his homestead for some years, but a petition in June 1893 asked for it to be moved to a more central position. This petition carries seven names from Willinga (H. Gillard, W. Casey, T. Casey, G. Veitch, R. Innes, T. Ball, and one other), confirming the settlement there in the period 1889–1893. Postmasters in the period 1905–1913 included Eliza Hockey, Annie Boag (who offered to take it on, as well as teaching), George Veitch, G. W. Smith and W. Went.

There is a record of Arthur Baxter carrying the mail between Ulladulla, Termeil and Kioloa in 1891, on horseback, for £31 a year. At Kioloa, E. T. Mackay applied for the 'postmastership' in a letter dated 9 August 1889. He stated: 'my residence is in the same enclosure (a 30 acre paddock) as Messrs Goodlet and Smith's sawmill and the workmen's dwellings. I have been seven years in their employ and acted as postmaster at Redhead.' I am not sure if he was appointed. An office at Kioloa was opened some time before November 1912, when it was converted from a 'Receiving Office' to an 'Allowance Post Office' with Mr W. Walker as postmaster. Walker continued until the property was sold to Mrs London in 1929, after which the office was run by her sister Bernice ('Bobbie') Moore, and then her daughter Joy. The Kioloa office closed on 31 August 1976.

The first postmistress at Bawley Point appears to have been Mabel Wright, who started on 8 January 1910. She was succeeded by Mrs E. Hockey, who resigned in November 1911, handing over to Mrs Christina Vider, wife of the mill manager. My mother probably took over from Mrs Vider around 1919, and was postmistress until around 1939. The post office closed 31 July 1962.

The telephone was connected to both Bawley Point and Kioloa some time after the post offices opened. At Bawley Point the only phone was at the post office for many years, but in the early 1920s two subscribers (Collins at Guy's Willinga property, and Orr at Murramarang) were connected, necessitating an imposing and complex switchboard.

---

21 Information from Australian Archives, Sydney Office.

We take the phone so much for granted these days that we forget it was once a newfangled gadget, and that it took some getting used to. At Kioloa in the early days Mrs Walker would take off her apron and tidy her hair before answering the phone.

The Walker family came to Kioloa in 1910, and became a significant influence in the district. William Walker (1875–1938) had come from England in 1887 with his family.[22] He established a coconut plantation in the New Hebrides for his brother-in-law, Hepburn McKenzie. On 9 March 1910, McKenzie, in the name of his wife Helen Mary McKenzie, bought the Kioloa property from William Evans for £3,100. He asked Mr Walker to run the property for him, and to be 'bush manager' for the new mill, that is to supervise the cutting and hauling of the timber.

Figure 24: The Hamon's house, which also served as the Bawley Point Telephone Office. Alma Hamon is fifth front on the right (in light coat) with Bruce Hamon in front.
Source: Bruce Hamon.

---

22 Norton, H. G. *Finetta: A Family Saga 1791–1987*, H. G. Norton, Seaforth, NSW, 1987, p. 81.

William and Maud (1878–1967, née Brown) Walker and their two eldest children, Lillian and Roland, moved down to Kioloa in 1910. The house being built for them at the top of what was later called 'The Avenue' was not ready, so they stayed around three months with the Evanses at Murramarang House after first rejecting an old and bug-ridden hut near the mill site — the only building left over from the days of the Goodlet and Smith mill. During this period, Mrs Walker stayed in Milton, where her third child Isabel (Belle) was born. Her husband visited by bicycle from Murramarang — no mean journey on the awful tracks that passed for roads at the time.

When they moved into their own home, Mrs Walker found the surrounding bush oppressive, so trees were cleared from a strip running east from the house, giving a view of the sea over the sandhills. Around six houses were built soon afterwards along one side of the strip and facing south. These housed some of the employees for the new mill, and the area became known as 'The Avenue'. My grandfather, William Hamon, worked on the construction of the houses.

The Walkers had four more children: Ruth, Jean, Phyllis and Annie; the latter lived for only 10 days. Belle (Mrs J. C. Vider) and Lillian (Mrs V. Veitch) lived in Ulladulla most of their lives, and Phyllis (Mrs J. P. Ferguson) lived there after World War II.

William Walker, a lay preacher in the Methodist church, held services in the small school building near his house. This building was also used for entertainment: he had a hand-cranked movie projector, and showed mainly humorous items which came from Melbourne. Belle Vider recently gave me the following poem, written by her father; it captures the excitement of simple pleasures in places where there was little other entertainment:

WALKER'S PICTURE SHOW
We went to Walker's picture show, and Lor! it was a sight
For everyone in town was there, both black and white.
We went to see them pictures so everybody said,
Mothers had to take their kids, they wouldn't go to bed.
You talk about excitement, it licked the Aussie's fleet,
The people thought it bosker, and never could be beat.
They seemed to love the pictures and said it's worth a sprat
For that there clever picture man who runs a show like that.
Kids that hadn't cut a tooth, not three months old I'll swear
Sat gazing at them pictures as only kids can stare.
When kangaroos and elephants came trotting on the scene
Those nippers tried to catch them, 'twas the funniest thing I've seen.

> But when the show was ended, as every show must end,
> We all went home and, sad to say, with sixpence less to spend.
> But if the picture man will come and give another show
> We'll have another sprat's worth — it's worth it, don't you know!

Mr Walker took his 'picture show' to Bawley Point and Termeil. He enjoyed the shows as well as anyone, even to the extent of laughing so much at times that he could not continue to crank the projector.

But some entertainments were not in his line. While he was away from Kioloa on business, a dance was held in the school. It was a great success, and some time after his return he was approached for permission to hold another dance there. He replied: 'Not on your life. It took me a fortnight or so to sweep the devils out after the last dance.' Some dances were held in the feed shed down near Kioloa mill. Mr Walker had to go to these, whether he liked to or not, as the feed would still be in the shed, piled up at one end, and bullockies with a few drinks aboard would try to steal it. One resourceful bullock driver bored a hole through the floor of the shed, up into the feed, then collected it as it drained through.

Mr Walker was one of the earliest to use motor vehicles in the district. He started with motorcycles. The first was described by Charlie Stephens as 'an old Italian one, an F. N. (Fabrico Nationale or some bloomin' name)'. After this 'blew a piece out of the cylinder', Charlie was asked to take it to Ulladulla and send it to Sydney. Mr Walker got another motorcycle, a six horsepower Zenith, which he rode to Braidwood and back in one day,[23] but later changed to cars: first a T-model Ford, then a 'Standard'. Belle Vider recalls that the car could not be used at all for the first six months, due to heavy rains. I remember it making a drunken track in the rain-wetted, sticky unmade road past Murramarang School. To avoid crossing Willinga Lake, Mr Walker initially used part of 'Smart's Road', which apparently ran north from Durras Mountain to join the Bawley Point — Termeil Road at 'The Gap'. This meant leaving his vehicle in the bush, probably near Don Moir Hill, and walking the rest of the way to his home. Later, with help from others at Kioloa who were getting their first cars, he made a road from Murramarang around the head of Willinga Lake to the Bawley Point — Termeil Road at 'The Boiler'. It was a do-it-yourself age, even to the extent of making your own roads. I knew this road round the head of the lake well, and often used it when guiding guests in to my mother's guest house at Bawley Point.

---

23 *Ulladulla and Milton Times*, 31 December 1914.

Mr Walker also had an early radio receiver in the 1920s. Almost the only station that could be received in Kioloa was 2FC, which has now become Radio National. He was an enthusiastic listener, and would hurry back even from fishing to avoid missing a favourite programme.

Crops (corn, sorghum, oats) were grown to feed the bullocks and horses. There were 18 bullock teams used in connection with the mill work. Potatoes were also grown. Mr Walker ran a small store, mainly for the benefit of the mill workers. Being postmaster, minister, storekeeper and entertainer, he was undoubtedly the local community leader, and was well respected.

World War I had little direct effect on our area and its community. Both sawmills were working, although Kioloa mill burned down before the war ended. Timber-getting and milling were part of the war effort, so enlistment was not encouraged. Those who enlisted were given a send-off at Termeil, and each was presented with a wristwatch. The declaration of war must have been especially hard for those who had come from 'the old country'. Mrs Bevan recalls that her mother, Mrs Hogg, was very distressed when she opened a paper and saw the announcement. She wanted to go home to Scotland straight away, but was persuaded to stay at Bawley Point, a place she had regarded as 'the end of the earth' when the family had arrived there a short time earlier.

Bob Backhouse, who was living at Kioloa and working in the mill, enlisted and was killed. Mr Beattie, teacher at Bawley Point, also enlisted when war broke out. Belle Vider (née Walker) recalled that their family at Kioloa did not suffer any great hardship during the war. Her sister Lillian remembered having to go to bed early because they relied on petrol for lighting, and there was a petrol shortage. With no wireless, and only one or two papers a week, they did not hear much about the outside world. Some of the feeling of isolation at the time can be captured from the following verse, written by Mr Walker and published in the *Milton Times*:

> When the Kaiser and his mighty armies come to take our land,
> And they march along on sunny streets with the good old German band,
> The Kaiser he won't smile at me 'cause I'll be far away
> Where there ain't no streets and soldiers and 'no nothing' so they say.
> If he wants to find my residence it ain't on the map,
> So it's no good him looking for this nervous little chap.
> No doubt for sickly people it's a place where you should stop,
> Especially when the Kaiser and his guns begin to pop.
> Let me recommend to any who may suffer from the pip,
> Who ain't too keen on Germans or a European trip,
> Who are looking for a peaceful life upon a peaceful shore,

Where soldiers brave are never seen or canons loudly roar.

They seek dear old Kioloa where peace and safety dwell.

It may take a year to find it. When you do, Oh well,

You will never sigh for heaven or that other place many dread,

For you feel somehow you are living with a tombstone on your head.

Hepburn McKenzie came to Australia from Scotland as a single man, and started a timber mill at Pyrmont. He moved the company's head office to Glebe Island, and had timber yards at Belmore and Ryde. The company expanded after he took over a timber yard at Rhodes. McKenzie also had timber interests in New Zealand, and he imported timber from America to be cut in local mills.

His property at Kioloa was in his wife's name (Helen Mary McKenzie in the legal documents, but known to the Walker family only as 'Auntie Nellie'), and consisted of the 'front block' of 860 acres (block E on Map 1; presently the Edith and Joy London Foundation) and a 'bush block' of 1,600 acres (blocks H and G). It was bought from William Edward Evans on 9 March 1910, and was sold to William Walker on 9 December 1927, for the nominal sum of 10 shillings.

Before Kioloa mill started, McKenzie had employed teamsters to bring logs to the beach and load them onto the South Coast trading boats. The logs were hauled through the surf by means of winches on the beach and on the boat. Bullocks on the beach pulled the wire and slings into the shore. The boat's winch would wind the wire back, and the logs would be pulled through the water and hoisted over the ship. They were then lowered into the hold or onto the deck.

The medical needs of the community at Kioloa in the early days of McKenzie's mill were taken care of as far as possible by a Nurse Taylor. It was rare for the doctor to be called out from Milton; if he did come it would be a slow trip by sulky, or if the timing suited he might come to Termeil by service bus and be met there by sulky. Charlie Stephens, who as a young lad was driving a delivery cart for the Milton bakery, remembered being asked to take a sick child and its mother to the doctor in Milton. The mother was Mrs Gleeson, wife of one of the mill workers at Kioloa. They were past Termeil and going slowly since the horses were tired, when Charlie glanced at the child:

> the little kiddie was sort of staring at me, her eyes wide open, but she didn't seem to be right to me, because I tell you I had never seen any person dead in my life. And I said to Mrs Gleeson 'I think the little baby's dead Mrs Gleeson' and she let out a squeal or screech which you can quite understand.

They hurried on, but Dr Renwick pronounced the child dead when they arrived. The sad trip had taken about seven hours.

The following paragraphs summarise items of local interest in the *Ulladulla and Milton Times*, for the years 1891–93 (its first years of publication) and 1895–99.[24] 'Walinga' or 'Willinga' is referred to as a place separate from Bawley Point (for example, 25 February 1893, 29 April 1893). The locality referred to was near the north end of the tramline bridge over Willinga Lake. In the 1920s, we called this area 'The Lemon Trees'; it had been settled up to around 1920, and the horses used on the tramlines were stabled there (see Chapter 8).

Kioloa mill is considered to have started around 1884, and Bawley Point mill some years later. There is some indirect evidence on starting dates in the *Times*. In February 1893, Kioloa mill was said to have been in its present position, after the move from Red Head, for 'about nine years'. This puts the starting date at around 1884. For Bawley Point, the only clue from these issues of the *Times* seems to be the mention of the tramline from Termeil to Bawley Point being already in use in 1893 (24 June 1893).

Termeil is described as 'only in the early stages of development' in 1893 (24 June and 1 July), but there is little else to indicate its probable date of settlement. An article on the opening of the church at Termeil in the issue of 13 November 1897 mentions that Mr Herne settled there 11 years previously. This puts the settlement not later than 1886. The pioneering spirit was alive and well in the district. The *Times* of 24 June 1893 said of Termeil:

> The primeval forests — and some first-class timber is to be met with on all hands — are slowly disappearing, and already a good deal of open country is to be seen on every side. The pioneers of settlement and civilisation are wrestling with wild Nature, and slowly but surely man is gaining the supremacy, so that before long the giant trees and luxuriant undergrowth will have given way to rich pastures and artificial grasses, on which dairy herds will feed, and struggling, hard-working, patient selectors will develop into, let us hope, prosperous and well-to-do farmers. The small band of settlers at Termeil have already done much pioneer work, but much still remains to be done.

The following are some dates of events relevant to Bawley Point mill:

24 June 1893: The mill is working, and the tramline to Termeil is operational.

2 November 1895: Mill is working half time; the men are poorly paid. (There was a severe recession in the 1890s.)

30 May 1896: Mill shut down.

26 June 1897: Wreck of the *Bonnie Dundee*. Presumably the mill was working at the time; otherwise it is unlikely that the ship would be there, unless to unload goods.

---

24 From the film copies in the Mitchell Library, Sydney.

21 August 1897: Both Bawley and Kioloa mills are closed, but it is not clear if the closure was recent or not.

30 August 1897: Fire destroys the mill, or at least part of it. The account of this, on 4 September, leaves no doubt the mill was working at the time. It is hard to square this with the statement two weeks earlier that the mill was closed.

2 October 1897: Re-erection of the mill is under way.

27 November 1897: Mill has now been re-erected, and milling operations are being recommenced.

Considering the isolation, sparse settlement and poor roads, there was an impressive social life: cricket, dances, picnics, a literature and debating class (27 October 1899).

The short note on Kioloa on 4 February 1892 depicts an active social life there, including a local paper, the *Kiola Star*. This paper, handwritten and double-sided, and thought to have appeared weekly, had ceased two years before, 'when Mr and Mrs Pearson went to England'. (Mr Pearson had been mill manager.) Some copies of *Kiola Star* must have survived till recently. The following is reproduced from *Australian National University News*:

> Extracts from the *Kioloa Star* … show that Kioloa was a centre for shipbuilding, mining, champagne-making, as well as sawmilling. There was even a bathing establishment. The newspaper contains shipping notices, railway notices and letters complaining about the impassibility of the road to Milton and calling for a public meeting to be held at the town hall.
>
> The paper also recalls a picnic when a boat, *The Dancing Wave*, was chartered for Brush Island, leaving Railway Wharf at 9.30 a.m. and arriving at The Cove at 11 a.m. An awning was erected, officers lit the fires and the ladies provided the food.
>
> After food the botanizing party went towards Azure Bank. The hunting party, with guns and ammunition, set off for Mt Ocean View. They were scarcely at the top when a gigantic herd of gazelles started with all the speed of terror from the caves. Two fine animals were secured, one taken alive. A large party left in the afternoon and secured a large haul of schnapper.
>
> The 'Wanted' advertisements show the homestead, 'Sandbank', asking for a housekeeper; the shipbuilding company calling for tenders to complete the SS *Durras*; 'Oak Villa' wanted a skiff and 'The Stables' a cat.

Termeil seems to have been the most active centre, with its hotel and church both opening during the decade. It also had a post office, hall, butchery and store. The church was on the east side of Princes Highway, opposite the school. It was moved up the coast later. The hotel, under Hugh Bevan, opened in August 1892. Termeil had a small hall early in the 1920s.

The main sport mentioned was cricket. This seems to have been played year round, if we can judge by the report on 13 July 1895. Racing is also mentioned (18 March 1893). Football came later: the *Nowra Leader* of 11 July 1913 records that Kioloa footballers travelled by steam launch from Bawley Point to play Milton.

The main industry was certainly the milling of timber at Kioloa and Bawley Point. Logging must have provided extra employment and income, particularly for residents of Termeil (24 June 1893). Dairying was also important at Termeil (3 December 1898), where a government dairying inspector found the best-conditioned cattle on the properties of A. Baxter, W. Herne and J. Evans, and at 'McKay's farm', between Kioloa and Durras (25 February 1893). From the context, this was probably the farm on Durras Mountain, later worked by the Beadman family. There is mention of wattle-bark stripping (9 April 1898). Gold was mined in the district, the main places mentioned being Currowan, Bimbramalla, Nelligen and Batemans Bay, and at least a rumour of alluvial gold in the centre of Termeil (17 August 1895). Fine gold in the black sand on Murramarang Beach is also mentioned (4 April 1896). Murramarang gets little mention. The brief reference on 25 February 1893 indicates Mr W. Evans had the property, and was running cattle there.

Figure 25: Kioloa rugby football team, c. 1910.
Source: The Edith and Joy London Foundation of The Australian National University.

Not much is said about supplies, but the report on Kioloa in the 4 February 1892 issue implies most supplies came by ship. The 'truck' system at Bawley Point (see page 58) also implies that the goods supplied in lieu of wages would have been sent by the company's ship.

There was a tragic drowning in Willinga Lake on the afternoon of 8 October 1895, when two teenage daughters of John Lynn, manager of Bawley Point mill, lost their lives. The girls were Sarah, aged 16 years and seven months, and Henrietta, aged 15. The following note, from the 19 October 1895 issue of the *Times*, gives some details:

> *Late Bathing Fatality at Willinga Lake: A True Heroine*
> The Rev. J. Hornby Spear writes: 'In justice to the memory of a brave girl, permit me to mention a fact in connection with the late deplorable accident at Willinga Lake, which did not come out at the inquest, owing to the illness of my informant, Annie Bettens, the sole survivor of that ill-fated pleasure party. The three girls, Sarah and Henrietta (Etta) Lynn and Annie Bettens, were in the water for over half-an-hour, when "Etta" Lynn got out and was about to dress when her attention was attracted to the two girls, Sarah Lynn and Annie Bettens, screaming for help; and looking round she saw that they had got into deep water and were sinking. Without a moment's hesitation, or thought of self, the brave girl sprang back into the lake and caught her sister Sarah by the arm and Annie Bettens by the shoulder; unfortunately the convulsive gasps of the drowning girls caused her to lose her balance, and she also was dragged into deep water and lost her life. The two sisters were subsequently found with their arms clasped around one another's neck, a sufficient evidence of the hopelessness of their chance of escape. Annie Bettens kept herself afloat by paddling with her hands until the brave boy Wagstaff swam out to her rescue. These facts I learned at the bedside of Annie Bettens, the sole survivor, and surely they ought to be known so that a well-merited word of praise might be paid to the memory of that brave, unselfish and noble girl, Henrietta Lynn, who gave so signal and heroic an example of the "Greater Love" (John XV. 13) by the shore of Willinga Lake.'[25]

Several children died from diphtheria; apparently the very sparse settlement provided no safety. There was no hospital (15 January 1898), so accident victims needing continued care had to be taken in by private families. A doctor was resident in Milton.

The poor state of the roads, especially the road linking Termeil, Bawley Point and Kioloa, was often mentioned.

---

25 *Australian National University News*, Vol. 10, No. 1, May 1975, p. 11.

CHAPTER 6
TRANSPORT: SHIPS AND ROADS

Ships provided the earliest connection between Sydney and South Coast ports. It was a tenuous lifeline, at the mercy of the weather at open places like Bawley Point and Kioloa, but it did not require the large outlay of time or capital needed for roads and bridges.

We have few details of the earliest ships that might have served Murramarang. Presumably many also served ports further south. These are graphically described by Gibbney as 'a mosquito fleet of sailing craft ranging from cutters of seven or eight tons to barques, brigs and top-sail schooners of seventy or eighty tons'.[1] They carried anything they could, including passengers. A passenger who made the trip to Sydney in the 1830s on the cutter *Industry* recalled:

> [The trip] lasted a week with standing room only. The fifteen passengers were only able to sleep in turns. To keep its complement in rations, the ship had to call at every trace of civilisation on the coast and all meals had to be taken ashore to enable passengers and crew to cook the inevitable damper.[2]

Another glimpse of the poor transport in the early years comes from Mrs Rose, who as a young girl lived at Moruya where her father was overseer for Mr Campbell in the late 1830s:

---

1   Gibbney, H. J. *Eurobodalla: History of the Moruya District*, Library of Australian History, Sydney, 1989, p. 40.
2   ibid., p. 40.

There was only one sailing vessel, named *Waterwitch* or *Wonderwitch*, that called at Broulee about once a month, bringing provisions from Sydney, and the shortage was at times acute. Aboriginals saved the settlement several times from starvation by supplying fish and oysters.[3]

Although steamships began to replace sailing ships on the South Coast as early as 1840, there was overlap for many decades.[4] I was surprised to find that all the ships referred to in the 1890s as visiting Bawley Point, Kioloa and Durras to load timber were sailing ships. I had known only steamers in the 1920s, but these were relative latecomers, the ones I knew (*Bermagui*, *Narani* and *Bergalia*) starting no earlier than around 1912.[5]

The shipping service was taken for granted, so only the ships that got into difficulties were mentioned. The *Bonnie Dundee* was wrecked at Bawley Point on 19 June 1897. The local paper reported the event:

> Wreck of the *Bonnie Dundee* at Bawley Point
>
> Crew Saved: Narrow Escape for Captain
>
> On Thursday night, 17th instant, a heavy chop sea from the north-east was running. The *Bonnie Dundee* was riding at anchor abreast Mr Guy's mill. Fears were entertained for her safety, those on board being on watch through the night. At times the sea broke clean over her. At four o'clock on Friday morning, the moorings parted, and in a very short time the unfortunate vessel was on the rocks. With some difficulty a line was got to the shore, and the hands succeeded in reaching the land in safety, with the exception of the Captain, who could not be persuaded to leave her, and Mr Walter Mackay volunteered to go to his rescue. At this time Captain Giddens was not to be seen on the vessel, and young Mackay was none too soon in his rescue. He found the Captain in an exhausted state on the weather side, the *Bonnie Dundee* being broadside on to the breakers. With some difficulty he got him safe ashore. It is expected the *Bonnie Dundee* will be a total wreck. Had the sea not moderated she would have broken up quickly. Mr Guy is the owner, and I am given to understand the vessel is insured for 400 pounds.
>
> Later: Since writing the foregoing, the *Bonnie Dundee* has completely broken up. Portion of her bows is all that remains sticking out of the water.[6]

They must have been especially unlucky with the weather, as strong north-easters are unusual in winter. From the above account of the wreck, it is not clear where the ship finally broke up. I remember finding some anchor chain

---

3   Rose, C. A. 'Recollections of the Early Days of Moruya', *Journal of the Royal Australian Historical Society*, 8, 1922–23, p. 375.
4   Andrews, G. *South Coast Steamers*, Marine History Publications, Sydney, undated, p. 9.
5   ibid., p. 30.
6   *Ulladulla and Milton Times*, 26 June 1897.

near the seaward end of Cockatoo Rocks, at the south end of Bawley Point Beach, and wondering how it got there. The *Bonnie Dundee* was built at Macleay River, NSW, in 1876. Dimensions: 84 tons, 85.2 x 19.3 x 7.8 feet.

Earlier (9 February 1895) the *Times* reported that the schooner *Hilda* had been blown ashore at Bawley Point, presumably onto the beach, and landed high and dry without any damage. She was still there a week later, but it was hoped she would be re-floated. She was flat-bottomed, so probably a scow rather than a schooner, which made it easier to jack her up so skids could be put underneath. There were no further references, so presumably she was returned to duty. Loney records the loss of a vessel named *Hilda* at Wreck Bay, 30 July 1908.[7] This was probably the same vessel. Details: Built 1891; wooden scow, 65 tons; dimensions 86.2 x 21.8 x 4.4 feet.

Another vessel which visited Bawley Point in the 1890s was the *Molinger*, mentioned in the local paper on 11 March 1893 in connection with an accident on board: the mate 'got jammed while stowing a long beam in the hold'.[8]

The schooner *Gleaner* — 115 tons, employed in the timber trade — was wrecked at Bawley Point on 20 May 1900. She carried a crew of six and was valued at £900. She was built at Hobart in 1870, and was owned by Mr Guy.[9]

To complete the list for Bawley Point, Mr Bill Cullen recalled in 1975 that his father had spoken of the wreck of a sailing ship called the *Arab*. The crew tried to get ashore in one of the ship's boats which was to be lifted by the crane. It was night, and the lifting did not go as planned; the human load was tipped into the sea. Local mill workers, many of them Aborigines,[10] helped fish out the unfortunate crew. Bill Cullen thinks one person might have been drowned. The Cullens lived at Bawley Point for 17 years; this would probably be 1905–1922. Mr Cullen senior was engine driver and fireman at the mill.

There were several wrecks at Kioloa. The schooner *Samoa* was driven onto Butler's Point during the night of 6 July 1893 and became a total wreck.[11] She was an old craft, formerly used in the slave trade, but had recently been refitted by her owners, Goodlet and Smith, who also owned Kioloa mill at the time. The crew were rescued by lifeline between 5 and 7 a.m., Captain Books

---

7   Loney, J. K. *Australian Shipwrecks: Including vessels wrecked en route to or from Australia, and some strandings*, Marine History Publications, 1987, Vol. 4, p. 49.
8   ibid., Vol. 3, p. 280.
9   *Ulladulla and Milton Times*, 26 May 1900.
10 Aboriginal men were a large part of the timber industry workforce from the early twentieth century, working in the mills and in the forests. They were highly regarded for their skills throughout Victoria, NSW and Queensland. Aboriginal family oral traditions have many references to their men working in the sawmills on the South Coast, crossing many generations. Yet, there is little in the written records. It is a story yet to be written (A.G. and S.F.).
11 *Ulladulla and Milton Times*, 8 and 15 July 1893.

being the last to leave the ship. According to Loney, the anchor chain parted in a heavy sea, and the wind was too light to get her under way.[12] Details: built Stockholm 1866; wooden vessel of 163 tons; dimensions 112.3 x 25.2 x 11.1 feet.

The *Wyoming* — a steamer of 258 tons gross and dimensions 132 x 23 x 10.3 feet — was wrecked on the night of 28 October 1910. This wreck was due to engine failure as the ship was about to enter Kioloa between Belowla Island and O'Hara Head. The ship struck the rocks within five minutes, and broke up completely within 24 hours. The crew landed safely on the beach.[13] Belle Vider (née Walker) said the captain and crew of the *Wyoming* stayed with the Walkers after the wreck. The captain gave her father the ship's barometer, which her brother had for many years.

Neil Evans recalled seeing the steering wheel of the *Wee Clyde* when he was after lobsters near the Kioloa mill site, but I have no details of the vessel or its wreck. Another source says a vessel called *Wee Clyde* was built at Narooma in 1909 for the Clyde Sawmilling Company, and burnt at its moorings in 1935.[14] In the 1920s, George Moore collected copper sheeting from the old beams of a wreck in this area.

Reg and Innes Collins mentioned the wreck of the trawler *Montgomery* on Kioloa Mill Point (O'Hara Head), but did not know the date.

Brush Island and Wilford's Point have claimed a few ships over the years. The earliest appears to have been the barque *Camden*, which was wrecked between Brush Island and the mainland on 30 January 1870.[15] She was en route from London to Sydney with a cargo of 40 tons of pig iron and 2,909 deals, and was a wooden vessel of 235 tons built at Nantes (France) in 1850. Dimensions: 96.3 x 24.4 x 13.5 feet. The crew rowed one of her boats to the Clyde River for assistance; apparently they did not realise Murramarang was settled. Two smaller vessels, the ketch *Agnes and Henry* (25 tons) and the fore-and-aft schooner *Mary Cosgrove* (31 tons), were sent to recover some of *Camden*'s cargo, but went ashore at Murramarang during a gale on the evening of 19 February 1870, and became total wrecks. That summer must have been an open season for ships in the area. A vessel called *Bull Pup* is believed to have been wrecked near the small beach which now carries that name, but I have not seen any details.

A fishing boat owned by Tony Holt of Ulladulla capsized and sank around two kilometres east of Brush Island in November 1922.[16] Holt and his companion, Thomas Brown, a married man with five young children, swam towards the

---

12 Loney, J. K. op. cit., Vol. 3, p. 229.
13 *Ulladulla and Milton Times*, 5 November 1910.
14 Hudson, I. and Henningham, P. *Gift of God: Friend of Man*, Aust. Forest Ind. Jnl. Pty. Ltd., 1986, p. 84.
15 Loney, J. K. op. cit., Vol. 2, p. 220.
16 *Nowra Leader*, 17 November 1922.

island. Holt got ashore, but his companion did not. Holt then had to swim the channel between Brush Island and the mainland — an area with a bad reputation for sharks. He crossed safely, but it is said he gave a bad fright to two men who were panning for gold on Murramarang Beach. They raised their heads to see a naked man appearing out of the surf. They let him have some scanty clothing, and directed him to our house at Bawley Point, where he would be able to phone the police. I remember him coming to the back of the house, and I remember also the consternation with which his news was received.

Two part-Aboriginal brothers, who had been camping on Brush Island for fishing, disappeared in May 1933 and are presumed to have drowned. They were Charles William Thomas Brown, aged 21, and his brother Ezekiel Francis Patrick Brown, aged nine. A half-brother, Syd Lewis Duncan, had been camping on the island with them, but came ashore with fish to sell on 18 May. The Browns rowed back to the island. After some days of bad weather, Duncan returned to the shore opposite the island on 22 May, but did not get any response to his signals. He left, thinking the Browns were fishing on the other side of the island. The next day he returned and signalled again, but with no result. He went to the island with Frank Carriage of Bawley Point in Frank's boat, but they could not find any trace of the Browns or of their rowing boat. The police were called, but further searches on the island gave no clue. On the beach opposite the island, two oars and parts of the boat were found. No foul play was suspected.

The trawler *Athol Star*, owned by Les Bringhoff, was wrecked at Bull Pup Beach (east end) around 1950. The hull lay in the sand there for perhaps 20 years, an object of passing interest, especially to children.

The largest vessel wrecked in the area was the *Northern Firth*. She struck an uncharted reef near Brush Island on the afternoon of Sunday 21 February 1932. Water entered the engine room, disabling the engines. A strong north-east wind drove her onto the north-east corner of Brush Island, where she stuck fast and in the next few weeks became a total wreck. She had been carrying around 1,800 tons of general merchandise from Melbourne. Some of this drifted away from the ship and was washed ashore mainly to the south. Some, including spirits, was pillaged before a guard could be placed on the wreck. Due to the Depression, there was more than usual interest in scavenging and beachcombing. The *Northern Firth* was built in 1922 by Grangemouth Dockyard Co.: 1,954 tons gross; 1,163 tons net; dimensions 280.2 x 41.9 x 19 feet.[17] She was under charter to James Patrick and Co., Sydney.

---

17   Loney, J. K. op. cit., Vol 4, p. 140.

Figure 26: *Athol Star* wrecked on Bull Pup Beach, c. 1950.
Source: A. R. Settree, Huskisson, NSW.

Mrs Grace Jarman (née Kellond) said the Kellonds were living in Murramarang House at the time of the *Northern Firth* wreck. Captain McDonald stayed with them after the wreck. Billy Orr was also at Murramarang, living in the small dairy building to the south of the main house. He had the telephone, and I remember being told that the first local news of the wreck was a phone call to Orr late at night from one of the Sydney papers. Later some local residents remembered seeing the vessel on the afternoon of the wreck, and thinking she was a bit close inshore, and why wasn't she moving? A spot of fishing, perhaps? No one suspected she was aground.

Only one ship has been built in the area: the *Douglas Mawson*. Named after the Australian Antarctic explorer, she was built at Bawley Point and launched 11 April 1914. She was the largest of over 20 wooden ships built by A. W. Settree between 1902 and 1948 at various places on the NSW coast, between Tomakin and Tweed River.

6. TRANSPORT: SHIPS AND ROADS

Figure 27: *Northern Firth* wrecked on Brush Island, February 1932.
Source: The Edith and Joy London Foundation of The Australian National University.

These days we think of ships being built in well-equipped shipyards, so the building of a single ship in an isolated settlement is hard to understand. Why was it done that way? There were several reasons. It was built for A. & E. Ellis, timber merchants, who probably already owned the Bawley Point mill (see Chapter 4). It was easier in those days for the shipwrights, around eight in number, to go with their simple hand tools to a site near a mill, than to have timber cut and transported to a shipyard. The special hardware needed had to come from Sydney; this was easier by ship than by road. And it was very important for the shipwrights to have their say in the selection of timber in the forest, since so many pieces of special shape were required. The ship was built in the open, so no special large building was needed. Some official details of the vessel, from Lloyds Register (1918) and supplied by Ronald Parsons, South Australia, are:

> Wooden twin screw steamship, official number 136387, ketch rigged, i.e. two masts, one deck, 333 gross and 167 nett-tons. 141.6 x 30.7 x 7.8 [these would be length, breadth and draught, in feet]. Two compound steam engines by Chapman and Co., Sydney.

Good descriptions of the building methods current at the time are given in two recent books.[18] These books contain accounts of interviews with Alf Settree of Huskisson, NSW, son of the builder of *Douglas Mawson*. Here we give only a very brief outline of the tools and methods.

---

18   Kerr, G. *The Tasmanian Trading Ketch: An Illustrated Oral History*, Mains'l Books, Portland, 1987, pp. 37–8, 54–67; Kerr, G. *Craft and Craftsmen of Australian Fishing 1870–1970: An Illustrated Oral History*, Mains'l Books, Portland, 1985, p. 138. See also the Lady Denman Maritime Museum in Huskisson.

The timber used was spotted gum. It was stacked for three or four months to season after cutting. The timber was not steamed to make bending easier. Naturally shaped pieces of timber — about 500 of them, most from individual trees — were used for the frames. The planking would have been about 30 x 5 centimetres, or 30 x 7.5 inches, in places requiring extra strength. These planks were up to 15 metres long, and would weigh about 200 kilograms. But these were not the heaviest. The keel would have been about 45 centimetres square, and made up of two pieces 15–20 metres long, scarf jointed end to end. Each of these keel timbers would weigh over two ton. For extra strength a keelson was used, of similar size and structure to the keel. These very heavy timbers were too large to be milled, so they were cut by hand in the bush, no mean feat.

Figure 28: *Douglas Mawson*, built at Bawley Point, launched 11 April 1914.
Source: Bruce Hamon.

The main hand tools were the axe, broad axe, adze, drawknife, saw and auger. The planking would have been cut in the mill, but the other pieces were shaped by hand. Fastenings were bolts of brass or Muntz metal, but the deck was fastened with square galvanised spikes six inches long, called 'U-bangs'. Bolts for fastening the keelson to the keel could have been up to 1.5 metres long, and 30 millimetres in diameter.

Figure 29: *Douglas Mawson* under construction, Bawley Point, 1913.
Source: A. R. Settree, Huskisson, NSW.

The ground at the chosen building site, a few hundred metres east of the mill, had too much slope for the usual stern-first launching, so she was built roughly parallel to the shoreline and launched broadside. Many must have crossed their fingers when the time came. Alf Settree's grandfather is reported to have said: 'It will be a launching and a shipwreck as well!' But all went well, and the next day she was towed to Sydney by another Settree-built (and Ellis-owned) ship the *Our Elsie*, to be engined and fitted out. Mrs Bevan (née Hogg) was present at the launching:

> Mrs Settree launched the *Douglas Mawson*. The launching was a big day. It was the first time I saw two men fighting. Barrels of beer were everywhere, sitting on stumps and logs. I don't know who fought, many strangers were there. I remember crying and hanging onto mother's skirts. There were a Mr and Mrs Jones, he had been working on the boat, and had two sons, also working on the boat. I watched Mrs Jones putting cakes down her umbrella and then going up to the house.

The *Douglas Mawson* served the timber trade on the north coast for four years, then was sold to a group in West Australia. In 1918–20 she was back east, in the Newcastle coal trade, and was then sold to the Queensland government for work in the Gulf of Carpentaria. There she went missing with all hands in March

1923, a victim of one of the worst cyclones known in the area. Meteorologists still refer to the 'Douglas Mawson cyclone', so at least the name carries on, though the circumstances might have been happier.

The ships I remember at Bawley Point in the 1920s were all steamers, owned and operated by the Illawarra and South Coast Steam Navigation Co. Ltd. (usually referred to as the ISN Co.). The same ships also called at Kioloa. The ISN Company operated from 1904 to 1951.[19] Their fleet was referred to as the 'Pig and Whistle Boats', as they often carried pigs (and calves) in temporary pens on deck. The pens were just forward of the passengers' accommodation, so a slight headwind made life unpleasant for any passengers. The *Bermagui* (steel), *Bergalia* (steel) and *Narani* (wood) were all about 150 feet long, so they were roughly the same size as the *Douglas Mawson*. These three are the ones I remember most, as they continued calling at Bawley Point for timber for some years after the mill burnt down in 1922. The *Benandra* (wood) and *Bodalla* (wood), both wrecked in 1924, probably called also in earlier years.

The arrival of a ship was a great event. The ship's whistle was blown as she rounded the point, so men could be available to help make mooring lines fast to ring bolts set in the rocks. (An old chap at Kioloa decided to make his first trip to Sydney by ship. He was asked if he had anyone to meet him. 'No', he said, 'but they'll hear her blow!')

Three names of captains I can recall are Andrews, Jackson and Miles. We were especially friendly with Captain 'Billy' Andrews. He did shopping for us in Sydney, came ashore to visit while the ship was loading, and (I was told later) took me for walks when I was too young to venture out alone. We kept in touch with him in later years. He was a short man who spoke with a nasal twang caused by a broken nose early in life. He told me of strong ocean currents, especially near Jervis Bay, which could set either onshore or offshore. This seemed unlikely, but I found later that he was right: large anticlockwise eddies, when close to the coast, would account for such currents.

Large tins of dripping, from the ship's galley, were often brought ashore and shared by several families. I think we supplied fresh milk in return, but I cannot remember how it was transported; the usual open bucket seems an unlikely choice. The captains came ashore in a small dinghy, propelling it with a single oar at the stern. At Kioloa, the Moore family sold young wild parrots to the ship's crew, who resold them in Sydney. The crew provided ropes for climbing to the nests.

---

19   *Australasian Shipping Record*, May 1974.

With improved land transport, the ISN ships rarely carried passengers. My mother and I went from Bawley Point to Ulladulla once, on our way to Sydney, and Belle Vider made one trip from Kioloa to Sydney. I think the *Bermagui* was the only ship with any passenger accommodation.

What happened the Pig and Whistle Boats? *Bermagui* was one of only two ships still operated by the ISN Co. when it went out of business in 1952. At that time, she was handling timber from a restricted range of ports.[20] She was a mine sweeper during World War II. In 1955 she finally left Sydney, becoming a gravel barge on the Brisbane River, and later a gravel dredge. *Bergalia* ended up in Noumea where she was converted to a powered lighter, and was reported still in service under the name *Tiburon III* in 1974. *Bergalia* was the youngest of the three regular callers at Bawley Point, having been built following the loss of *Benandra* in 1924. *Narani* was also used as a mine sweeper during the war. In 1950 she went to New Guinea, where she was probably broken up around 1955.

Bergalia performed an unplanned but very welcome service in the district in her later years. She was tied up at the Ulladulla wharf when severe bush fires broke out in the district on 14 January 1939. Water was not laid on at the time, and things could have been much worse than they were if the ship's crew had not started the pumps and filled 44 gallon drums with sea water. The filled drums were taken by lorry to the fire fronts.

The history of roads in any area is hard to trace. They start as mere tracks, and are abandoned quickly and without record when a new route opens. Only the most successful and important are surveyed. Roads have been mentioned in earlier chapters, but here we try to summarise what little is known.

The earliest road in our area was almost certainly the road from Murramarang to Ulladulla, said to have been finished before 1837 (see Chapter 2). Although no route details were given in the one line statement that the road had been made, I believe this road was the one referred to in my school days as 'the old South Coast coach road', and which I could trace from north of Meroo Lake to at least Murramarang. It crossed the mouths of Willinga and Meroo lakes, and would have crossed Termeil, Tabourie and Burrill lakes in similar fashion. At the Willinga Lake crossing, stonework and fill were needed to grade the track up from the beach to Willinga headland. This stonework forms the base of the present rough foot track, and traces of the original stone wall can still be seen on the left side of the track going down. This wall was much more clearly visible in the 1920s. Although the track itself was also fairly obvious at that time, it was clear it had not been used for a long time, probably many decades.

---

20 ibid., May 1974, p. 139.

I doubt if this was ever a 'coach road', in the sense of a route for regular passenger coaches. It would have been put in for use by bullock drays or wagons, which could negotiate the stretches of beach sand without too much difficulty. It is likely the early settlers did not realise the lakes opened to the sea and could stay open for long periods. The sand banks, quicksand and tidal currents when the lakes were open must have presented many extra difficulties. It is not clear why the road was not routed around the heads of at least Willinga, Meroo and Termeil lakes, which are smaller than the other two. I suspect the route was chosen without much thought, and almost certainly without a proper survey.

This is almost certainly the track that the Rees Jones family would have taken on their way to and from Brooman through Murramarang in the 1840s (see Chapter 2). It is interesting that their route from Boro was via Nerriga, across towards Jervis Bay and south to Ulladulla, Murramarang and Brooman. There was no direct vehicle route from Braidwood to the coast at that time. Mrs Jones mentions that they travelled along the sea beaches, taking advantage of the firmer sand near the water. This was done both north and south of Ulladulla, and under very trying conditions in hot weather. At one stage on their way north, and probably on Tabourie Beach, they were 'desperately hungry and faint … but on, on we went, hour after hour, mile after mile, still keeping along the beach'. They were very grateful to find a lot of fish stranded in a water hole; some of these were taken with them to 'Garrett's farm', where they stayed the night. This is believed to be the farm of the Garrad family near Milton, Garrad having been Stephen's first overseer at Murramarang. The Garrads were grateful for the fish, as they were nearly out of food, and were reduced to eating parrots.

Figure 30: Old coach road, 1988.
Source: Margaret Hamon.

The next mention of the road is by a correspondent for *Town and Country Journal* in 1870. He was on horseback, but referred to 'the dray track on the margin of the Meroo' (see Chapter 3). 'Dray track' seems a more appropriate name than 'coach road'. The purpose of this road was so that the better harbour facilities at Ulladulla could be used, but it was apparently not fully successful, as some Murramarang produce was still being shipped from Kioloa in 1843 (see Chapter 2).

A direct road from Murramarang to Brooman, marked 'R1119a R', is shown on maps of Termeil and Albert parishes, but I have been unable to find any details or date. Most likely it was the route used by the Rees Jones family in the 1840s. I do not remember any mention of this road in the 1920s. The route shown on the parish maps is remarkably direct and smooth.

A surveyed road marked 'from Batemans Bay' and 'to Murramarang' appears on early survey maps of land portions on Durras Mountain (see Chapter 3). The route was up the north-east ridge and slightly west of the top of the mountain. I have seen no direct reference to the use of this road; it might have been the route used by the mailman mentioned by the *Town and Country Journal*'s reporter in 1870 (see Chapter 3), but this service was probably on horseback rather than by vehicle. There was no way for vehicles to cross the Clyde at Batemans Bay until the first punt in 1871; the power ferry did not start till 1915, and the bridge dates from 1956. The ferry at Nelligen started in 1875.

Figure 31: Collins' household goods being moved from Taralga to Willinga, 1919.
Source: The Edith and Joy London Foundation of The Australian National University.

After Termeil was settled, its link to Milton was via Monkey Mountain Road and Woodburn Road, as this route did not require any large bridges. It was often called 'the top road'. The route along the present Princes Highway developed in the 1890s and later. The well-built early road from near Flat Rock along the ridge west of Termeil, and marked 'old coach road' on the Tabourie 1:25,000 topographic map, would have avoided crossing even Termeil Creek (at the foot of Monkey Mountain), and may have been an alternative route into Termeil. At Flat Rock, a road branched to the south-west to Brooman and Shallow Crossing. This was presumably the preferred route to Batemans Bay and Moruya before ferry services started at Nelligen and Batemans Bay. Shallow Crossing's submerged concrete causeway was not put in until around 1930.[21]

Princes Highway was officially named in 1920, but at least parts were in use much earlier. It took a long time to earn the title of 'highway'. Belle Vider (née Walker) said their family bought a T-model Ford as their first car, and 'thought they were toffs'. They set out for a holiday at Blackheath, but between Milton and Nowra 'I don't think we travelled the main road once. We were going through the bush on side tracks.'

Nearer home, 'Smart's Road' has already been mentioned (see Chapter 5). This would have linked Durras Mountain (where Smart took up land around 1870), and possibly Kioloa, to Termeil. It appears to have been more inland than the present Kioloa–Bawley Point–Termeil road, and so would have avoided crossing Willinga Lake.

The tramline bridge was the earliest bridge over Willinga Lake, but it was unsuitable for vehicles, though one car did cross it in the early guest house days. From the start of Bawley Point mill until around 1932, vehicles coming from Termeil to Bawley Point crossed the lake near the site of the present bridge, or detoured from 'The Boiler' around the head of Willinga Lake to Murramarang. This detour was due to Mr Walker, so must have been put in after 1910. The lake bottom was firm enough, but you had to know and stick to an ill-defined J-shaped route where the water was shallow. Car drivers were advised to get out and walk through the lake first to check route and depth — no one thought to put up a depth indicator. Many cars stalled due to water in the engine, and had to be pulled out by bullocks or horses. This crossing was impassable after heavy rain, until the lake opened to the sea either naturally or with the help of many men with shovels.

---

21   *The Shoalhaven Telegraph*, Nowra, 14 August 1929.

6. TRANSPORT: SHIPS AND ROADS

Figure 32: Wooden bridge over Willinga Lake, c. 1960.
Source: Courtesy of the Dummett family.

The lake crossing affected horse-drawn vehicles as well as cars. Belle Vider recalled my father and grandfather (Henry Reynolds) trying to cross in a sulky to pick up supplies of bread and meat when the delivery truck could not get through. The horse jibbed in the middle of the lake, broke itself free and started off upstream. My father had no option but to go after the horse, up to his neck in water, much to the amusement of grandfather Reynolds. My father 'was that mad he felt like getting the shafts and tipping Mr Reynolds and the lot into the lake!' Even horse riders could have trouble. My pony often jibbed at crossing the lake, but I must admit he was spoilt and needed little excuse to put one over me.

A vehicle bridge was built eventually, around 1932. It was a simple structure: logs laid on the bed of the lake parallel to the shore, stringers across these, and decking on the stringers. It was built by Jack Bevan and Frank Evans. My grandmother nicknamed the builders 'Daudlin' Along': a skit on 'Dorman and Long' who were building the Sydney Harbour Bridge at the time.

This first bridge was replaced or at least extensively repaired in 1943. Neil Evans worked on this, with help from one of the council's road maintenance staff. The present concrete bridge was opened on 16 April 1969.

Although the lake crossing was difficult, the Termeil–Bawley Point road itself was no more than a track for many years. In April 1893, the local *Times* reported: 'The road from Termeil to Wallinga is in a frightful state. On Monday last a gentleman's buggy got stuck in the mud, and a team of bullocks had to be got to extricate it.'

At Kioloa, roads were made and improved by the London family after 1929. Their first major effort was a road up the 'Dangerboard', along the track of the tramline from the mill. They first took up the disused tracks, using some as flooring joists when extending their house. They used existing bullock tracks where possible, and eventually extended the road west to Princes Highway, giving the district another alternative to the crossing of Willinga Lake. Later, a shorter route, now marked on the Kioloa map as 'Moore's Road', was made through the back of their property.

The early routes from Bawley Point to Kioloa crossed private property, and this meant gates or slip rails had to be opened and shut, and suitably cursed, by all travellers. There were even a few of the fiendish 'Queensland Gates' in the area; these were barbed wire fastened to a gatepost at one end and to a loose pole at the other; the pole sat in a wire loop around the other gatepost at the bottom, and was fastened at the top by a moving loop. It sounds simple, and of course it is simple, but perhaps we should leave the rest unsaid. Some gates remained for many years, being removed only after the road was properly surveyed and its land resumed.

Around this time (the 1920s and 1930s), the Forestry Department built many roads in State Forests.

According to Clark, the first regular coach service between Nowra and Bega began in 1893.[22] Run by R. T. Thorburn, it was quite a large undertaking, with 40 coaches and 150 horses. By this date, there were bridges over Tabourie and Burrill lakes. Lucy King gives a slightly earlier starting date (1890), at least for a service between Nowra and Moruya run by Barney McTiernan.[23]

---

22   Clark, A. (ed.) *Shoalhaven Dateline*, Shoalhaven Historical Society, Nowra, 1988, p. 11.
23   King, L. *The Timber Industry in the Southern Portion of the Shoalhaven Shire*, unpublished MS, Milton/Ulladulla Historical Society, No. M634.

CHAPTER 7
BAWLEY POINT IN THE 1920S

This chapter gives my earliest memories of Bawley Point. My parents (Les and Alma Hamon) moved to Bawley Point around Easter 1918, when I was less than a year old. I lived at Bawley during all my primary school years (1925–1930). My parents continued to live there after 1930, although I saw less of the place, being a boarder at St Patrick's College, Goulburn, 1931–1935, and then a student at Sydney University, 1936–1940. My father, who was born and reared in Milton, worked initially in the sawmill, and we lived in one of the houses that had been built on the mill lease site, presumably when the mill first started in 1891. Our house was nearest the mill.

After the mill burnt down in April 1922, most of the mill hands moved away from Bawley Point. We stayed on, with my father initially stacking and tallying timber cut at the Flat Rock mill and brought to Bawley Point for shipment. The roads in the district have been discussed in Chapter 6. The road to Termeil was an unmade track, which gave a lot of trouble, especially to visitors. Since it was often easier to make a detour around an obstacle (fallen tree, boggy patch) rather than fix the obstacle itself, the tracks became tortuous and ill-defined. Local knowledge was almost essential. When guests from Sydney first started coming, it was one of my jobs to meet them, usually at Termeil, and guide them in. Often I would ride to Termeil on my pony, then ride back in front of the car, giving directions with signs and shouts. At other times I walked up and had the rare thrill of a car ride, even if only standing on the running board!

We had no car or even a sulky of our own, so getting anywhere was a major problem. I can remember only one car in the Bawley Point–Kioloa district at the time I started school. This was owned by Mr Walker at Kioloa. I think it was a Standard. We did not own even a horse in the early years of the decade. My father often walked to Termeil, for example, to pick up medicine sent out from Milton on the mail car.

By modern standards we were very isolated, but we were better off in some respects. Grocery orders were delivered to the door once a week (Friday) from Blackburn's in Milton, and bread and meat twice a week. These deliveries continued on to Kioloa, and even to the farm on Durras Mountain in earlier years. Blackburn's delivery was by a wagon drawn by two horses, and driven by Mr Edwin ('Winnie') King. I have been told recently that a third horse was harnessed in front of the usual two for the pull up onto Durras Mountain. Bread and meat came by motor van (Afflick, butcher in Milton), but may have come by horse-drawn vehicle in the earlier years. If the bread and meat could not be brought right to the door, due to the lake being too deep, it was left in a tin shed on the Termeil side of the lake. I often collected it from the tin shed on my way home from school at Termeil.

Michael Anthony, originally from India, had a store in Ulladulla, and made a weekly trip to Bawley Point and Kioloa. He operated as a hawker, carrying goods with him from which customers could choose on the spot. Michael came initially by horse and cart, and stayed overnight in a shack near our home. Later he had a T-model Ford. He could not read or write, so he had to remember each person's credit purchases, and sometimes got my father to write them down for him. With today's emporia in mind, it is interesting to reflect on what a small selection of goods could be hawked around by horse and cart. I remember clearly his stock of fishing gear — it was all in a single tin, about 25 x 20 x 10 centimetres.

Pushbikes were rare; I suppose the wretched state of most tracks made bike riding as difficult as travel by car. My grandparents owned a horse and sulky from around 1925; this made us more mobile.

Our home was a simple four-roomed cottage, weatherboard on the outside and lined with pine. It had a corrugated iron roof on which heavy rain drummed a merry tune. Perhaps the cottage was a little more than four-roomed: we had the post office, which was housed in a small room at the western end of the verandah. The post office served also as my bedroom, at least for some years. There was also a small room, the 'wash house', off the back verandah. This was really a toolshed and store for feed for the cow and poultry.

7. BAWLEY POINT IN THE 1920S

Figure 33: The Hamon's cottage and telephone office c. 1930. The extended house also served as the original guest house.
Source: Bruce Hamon.

The main rooms were all small, probably not more than 3 x 3 metres. I noticed the smallness particularly when I revisited the house in later years, not long before it was abandoned. Of course the rooms did not seem small to a child's eyes at the time. The building was similar in size and general layout to the cottages in The Avenue on the Edith and Joy London Foundation property at Kioloa.

There was no bathroom. Baths were taken in a galvanised iron tub on the kitchen floor, using water heated on the wood-burning cooking stove in a four-gallon kerosene tin. The stove had a fire-box on the left, oven on the right, and several removable circular plates on top. It boasted a few 'dampers' to control the draught. Mother worked wonders with this stove, but gave dad and me a 'time of it' if we didn't keep up a good supply of the various grades of firewood. Dad cut and split the heavier wood, while it was my job to collect sticks and bark for kindling, and to split lighter wood such as old palings for the next grade.

The kitchen had no built-in cupboards. There was a free-standing cupboard or safe which had a single shallow drawer near the top. Many of my childhood treasures were found in the 'kitchen drawer'. There were open shelves, covered with strips cut from newspapers. The down-hanging edges of these strips were scalloped and serrated. There were two small tables and a bench, covered with either oilcloth or pieces of linoleum. Water was drawn from a tap to the right of the stove, connected to tanks outside. There was no sink. Washing up was done in a dish, and the water thrown out onto the back lawn, or sometimes saved for the garden.

Life was very simple and amusements were few. In the evenings we often played cards. Five hundred was the favourite game, but euchre was also played. Billy Orr, who owned Murramarang, often visited to make up a four. We acquired a table model gramophone in the early '20s and had a lot of pleasure from it. I think it was bought for us in Sydney by one of the ship's captains, probably Captain Andrews.

We had little excitement and few crises. My father had a serious illness soon after we settled at Bawley, and had to be taken to Sydney. This must have been traumatic for Mother, but I was too young to remember it.

We had a near tragedy involving a shotgun when I was only about two or three years old. The gun had been left loaded, standing upright in a corner of the post office. The loading was deliberate: hawks or crows had been raiding the fowl yard and Mother was supposed to give them a blast or two if they came while Dad was at work. I was so young that it was assumed I could not even lift the gun, let alone do any damage with it. I did not lift it, but did manage with some effort to cock one barrel (it was a double-barrelled 12-gauge gun with hammers), and of course had no difficulty in pulling the trigger to see what might happen. Since the gun was standing upright the only damage was to the top of the linen press, and probably the roof. It took Mother and Father a long time to get over the thought of what might have happened. And it was a long time before I fired a shotgun again!

Much of our spare time was spent out of doors. The lake (Willinga, and sometimes Meroo) provided swimming and prawning. The most effective prawning was at night, using lights. We had a carbide cycle lamp which was fairly effective but temperamental. Hand or dip nets were used. During the day we got moderate catches of prawns by a method that seems to have died out. The prawns were raked out of the sand with a garden rake. Each disturbed prawn was followed till it settled and dug into the sand again when it was caught either by hand or with a dip net. A slow job but we kids had plenty of time. We explored the lake on rafts made of ships' hatch covers that had washed up on the beaches. These were too ungainly to row, but could be coaxed along with a pair of poles. I made one canoe out of a sheet of corrugated roofing iron. It was very unstable and leaked badly, but provided its share of fun.

Figure 34: Reg (left) and Innes Collins and their parents, Kioloa, c. 1932.
Source: The Edith and Joy London Foundation of The Australian National University.

Rabbit shooting with .22 rifles was my main sport. Rabbits were very plentiful; myxomatosis was still many years away. The rabbits were sometimes eaten but more often used to feed the cats. The skins were dried on wire frames and sold.

The beach provided much entertainment. We trundled hoops on the firm, wet sand at low tide, built the usual sandcastles, and had bonfires in the evenings. 'Bungers' were available free, in the form of the float bladders on seaweed. Surfing was not encouraged, at least not in the absence of the grown-ups. The first surfboards appeared around this time, brought I think by the Nicholsons. They were small flat rectangular boards, about 0.5 x 0.3 metres, which were held under the forearms. I had few playmates in the earlier years of the decade. There must have been many children in the families of other mill workers, but I do not remember them as the families moved away soon after the mill fire in April 1922. Frank Carriage was living near the Cullens for part of the time, and I got around (and fought!) with his son Willie, who went briefly to Murramarang School. The Carriages moved away, but Frank returned later with two younger children, Frankie and Charlie. Frank was a professional fisherman, and had an open boat with a small 'Chapman Pup' inboard motor. The boat was kept at the old mill site and launched by using the crane. That boat introduced me to the despair of seasickness. As well as boat fishing, mainly for snapper, Frank also netted Willinga and Meroo lakes, and I think also Murramarang lagoon, using a gill net.

The Hapgood family lived at Bawley Point. Olive was about my age, and we walked to Murramarang School together. Her sister Essie was younger, and I think the family moved away before Essie started school.

The only playmates who were around for the whole decade were Reg and Innes Collins — two kilometres away on Guy's Willinga property. We were together at Murramarang School for several years. The Collins family had come in 1919 to manage the property, and stayed till 1931. Several crops were grown on the property. I remember potatoes, maize (which was always called 'corn'), oats, artichokes (for cattle feed) and of course the watermelons that nearly did for me, and will be mentioned again later. They had a chaff cutter powered by a kerosene engine; some of the chaff was used to feed the horse teams working at Flat Rock. All the outside work such as ploughing was done with horses. Small dams were made using horse-drawn scoops. Some cattle were run, and sometimes the Collinses did their own killing. Guy owned property on Durras Mountain at the time, and ran cattle there, but I do not think anyone lived on the mountain after the Beadman family left around 1920.

Figure 35: Walter Scott at Willinga, probably c. 1930.
Note the extent of clearing.
Source: The Edith and Joy London Foundation of The Australian National University.

Lacking our own family transport, we did not often get away from home. Picnics involved carrying the necessities in sugar bags or hampers. Nuggan was a favourite place for picnics. Grandad Reynolds had built a substantial picnic table there under a large lilly-pilly tree.

7. BAWLEY POINT IN THE 1920S

We did not visit locally or entertain as far as I remember. We visited my grandparents on father's side in Milton (Wason Street) and sometimes visited friends in the Milton district. I recall particularly visiting George Claydon and Maude Cashman on a farm at Little Forest.

At home we had only kerosene lamps, with wicks but no mantles, in the earlier years. Later, especially after the guest house business started, we acquired an 'Aladdin' lamp (still kerosene and wick, but with a conical mantle), and a couple of petrol lamps that used mantles and had to be pumped. It was one of my jobs to keep these lamps filled, light them and replace mantles when necessary.

Washing the clothing and bed linen was done in the backyard, in the open. The wash load was boiled in a copper set in its own brick fireplace. After the boiling, the clothes were lifted from the copper with a 'pot stick' (about one metre length of broom handle) and transferred to tubs where most items were rubbed against a 'washing board' (square of wood with corrugated surface, about 30 x 30 centimetres, mounted in a frame so it would stand in a tub). So washing day meant hard work, and small boys found it convenient to be somewhere else if possible.

We kept a cow and fowls, and grew most of our own vegetables. Fresh fruit was scarce, except for locally grown peaches, nectarines, apricots, common lemons and apples. There was a small market garden at Kioloa about two kilometres inland from Merry Beach, run by a Chinese man (Chin Slin). He brought his produce round by horse and cart.

We did not have even an electric torch in the earlier years, and no radio until the late 1930s when I made a battery set for my parents. I recall one of our guests from Sydney bringing an early model radio, and the disappointment when it did not work.

Cats have been a part of my life as long as I can remember. The first I remember clearly was a fine tabby named Mit, who was born at our place when I was about three years old, and shared my earlier years. Mit was the most ticklish cat I have known, and I exploited this weakness with fiendish glee, using a pair of leather gardening gloves to even things up a bit. I was not cruel to him, but did not give him much peace. Mother was always at me to wash my hands after mauling the cat.

I had a dog for some years, but in retrospect I could have benefitted from some training in dog psychology. A dog's life was certainly a dog's life in those days, especially in the country. But he was a great companion when rabbiting and fishing, though he found the latter boring.

THEY CAME TO MURRAMARANG

A recent visit to the local barber reminded me that things were simpler and cheaper in the '20s. You did one another's hair, or else. Grandfather had a pair of hand clippers, which he kept well oiled; these were a boon compared to scissors. But there would be complaints from the customer if you did not keep squeezing those handles fast enough.

My mother was postmistress through the 1920s. The telephone was on a party line. Each exchange was identified by a particular ringing pattern. Ours was 'a long and a short'. Ringing was done by turning a handle — one turn for a 'short' and several turns for a 'long'. The party line connected a number of small exchanges, each of which might have a number of local subscribers. We had two subscribers: the Collins family on Guy's property one mile south, and Billy Orr at Murramarang. This small exchange system must have been installed around the middle of the decade; earlier we had only the simple wall-mounted phone. Other exchanges on our party line were Milton, Ulladulla, Termeil, Kioloa, East Lynne, Benandarah, and perhaps Morton and Flat Rock.

The phone line from Termeil to Bawley was a single unstranded galvanised iron wire strung through porcelain insulators which were tied to trees using the same kind of wire. We were provided with a pair of pliers, a wire strainer and some spare wire, and were expected to go out and fix the line after storms. Outages were frequent. A technician came occasionally to do an overall check and change batteries (four large 1.5 volt dry cells at each exchange). The replaced batteries usually had some life in them, and provided power for my earliest electrical experiments. One technician, Mr Dean, was very helpful in explaining the electrical mysteries to me. I learnt recently that he was killed in an on-duty accident at Wandandian.

A trunk call through to Sydney was difficult and time-consuming. I often had this job when guests were in the house. There were frequent allegations of phone operators listening in to conversations on the party line. One had only to lift the receiver from the hook. In fact, it was necessary to listen in this way before ringing, to make sure the line was free. There must have been a strong temptation to listen for longer than necessary.

The mail was taken to Termeil on horseback on Mondays, Wednesdays and Fridays by the mailman, Walter Scott, who lived at Kioloa. The mail, even if only a few letters, was carried in a large canvas mail bag tied with string and sealed with sealing wax. A figure of the Crown was imprinted into the hot wax using a seal supplied for the purpose. No chances taken with the mail!

7. BAWLEY POINT IN THE 1920S

Figure 36: Alma Hamon and 'Mit', c. 1930
Source: Bruce Hamon.

The guest house business at Bawley just happened without any planning. There are two versions of how it started. Mother's version was that she spoke to Dr Blaxland, an eye specialist in Macquarie Street, about the beauty of the place, and the fishing. He decided it would be a good place for a holiday and invited himself down, making little of Mother's protestations about lack of space. He came, enjoyed himself, then spread the news among friends, after which there was no turning back. The other version was told to me recently by Dave McCathie. He claims the guest house business started when Frank Sargent and party were camping at Bawley and were flooded out. They asked Mother to take them in. Probably both versions are true. The start would have been around 1925. I don't remember how many guests were accommodated at one time in the original small cottage, or what ingenuity was used to fit them in. I have a vague memory of many camp stretchers in different parts of the house. But space limitations quickly forced a decision to add extra rooms and a bathroom at the eastern end of the house. These additions were made by my father with help from Frank Carriage, and probably also grandfather Reynolds. The extended cottage served as guest house until the present guest house in Johnston Street was opened around 1932.

Mother, besides being the cook, was also the business manager. I often wonder how she managed with no electricity, no refrigerator, not even an ice chest in the earlier days, and only a pathetically small stove for cooking. The stove was supplemented by a single burner Primus stove, and a small kerosene stove with two parallel wicks. Mother was very attached to this wick stove, but few others could get it to cook or stop it smoking. Mother was an excellent cook, especially of fish. This was most often covered in egg and breadcrumbs and deep fried in oil, but large snapper might be stuffed and baked. Snapper soup was a specialty.

Figure 37: Bawley Point c. 1927, after the mill fire.
The feed shed (left), crane and chimney stack, and some mill buildings (including the blacksmith's shop) survived the fire. The first guest house, with the additional rooms on the left for the guests, and its extensive garden area, is above the corner of the beach. The dark line running left from the house towards the mill buildings is the tramline.
Source: Bruce Hamon.

Most guests enjoyed themselves and many came back year after year, becoming friends of the family. Ralph Johnston (a descendant of Major George Johnston, who had deposed Governor Bligh in 1808) must have come first around 1925. I remember him teaching me to dance on the front verandah, providing rubber bands for a catapult and joining enthusiastically in shooting and fishing trips. He settled at Bawley when he retired, and was one of the most loved identities in the district.

The guest house business must have influenced me in many ways. I had extra chores. Washing up was one I didn't like — who does? Mother was strict and had definite ideas that I didn't always go along with — such as washing and drying the bottoms of plates as well as the more obvious tops. Another chore was to take a bucket of milk each morning across the beach to Grandad's where I helped with separating the cream, using a small bench-mounted hand-turned separator. This short trip with the milk was at the time when guests and campers were enjoying their morning swim, so I felt especially annoyed that I could not join in.

I met many people and had my narrow horizons stretched in the process. I recall in particular Mr G. Haskins, at that time a senior engineer with the Sydney Water Board, explaining to me the difference between a professional engineer and a mechanic.

Here are the names of some of the early guests: Dave McCathie (McCathie's Ltd, Pitt St) and Mrs McCathie. They came in 1929, not long after their marriage, and eventually settled in the cottage at the north end of the beach. Several members of the Winn family (Winn's Ltd, Oxford St and Newcastle) (Mr Gordon Winn gave me a lift back to Sydney in his open-model Rolls Royce the day war was declared in 1939). Sir John Madsen, Professor of Electrical Engineering at Sydney University, and the best beach fisherman I ever knew. Mr H. H. Massie, remembered especially for his ability to tangle the heavy cord lines used when fishing for snapper from the rocks. F. H. Ernest Walker, architect. The Gardner 'boys', insurance brokers. C. H. Bell, dentist (and ventriloquist). Mr and Mrs F. V. Nicholson and their sons John and Frank, who stayed with my grandmother regularly twice a year for many years. Mr Nicholls, solicitor. C. W. Peck, author of *Australian Legends*, who enthralled us with stories as we sat near the kitchen stove on winter evenings. D. Brockhoff (Brockhoff's Flour, Glebe Road, Sydney). Jack Palmer (F. J. Palmer and Son, Sydney). Sid Ellis (son of a founder of the timber firm A. & E. Ellis) and family. Dr Spark, who liked fishing for sharks from the old gantry. Dr Blaxland, eye specialist, who probably started the whole business. E. Gallop (chairman of the Housing Commission). The anthropologists from Sydney (and Melbourne?); I am not sure of their names, but I seem to recall McCarthy, Towle and Thorpe. Doris Stenhouse and Marge Talbot (teachers, who came initially by bicycle in the late 1930s, became family friends, and later built a holiday cottage north of the guest house). Sir John McKelvey, surgeon. Dr H. Daly, anaesthetist. Dr Anderson-Stuart, radiologist. (These two were keen snapper fishermen, and both had cottages at Bawley later.) Captain Cooper R. N., who spoke severely to one of our cats: 'If you look at me like that, you'll get a thick ear!' The cat was not amused. Mr McFadyen, known to the girls as 'Mr Baby-Blue-Eyes'. Dr Ritchie. Mr Reg. Roberts.

In running the guest house, Mother had help from some of the local girls: Phyllis, Grace and Eileen Kellond, and Belle Walker helped at various times, and enjoyed it. As Belle put it: 'I loved helping my friend Mrs Hamon ... I loved it there, I had my own pony and I loved the fishing and I loved the land and I loved the place. For years I did that.'

Camping became popular during the 1920s. The favoured area at Bawley Point was among the trees on Willinga headland, but people camped anywhere that took their fancy. Water had to be obtained from local households, though some campers set up spear pumps in the sands near Willinga or Meroo lakes. There was no control or council supervision, nor any rubbish collection or toilet facilities. For the latter, you dug a suitable hole and put up a crude screen, usually of hessian, around it.

Most camps were one-family affairs, but Dr D. Bowman, a Paddington GP, did things on a much larger scale. Several families of relatives and friends were involved. Each family had its own tent, but there was a large dining marquee, and a separate cooking tent. Children under eight years were not allowed, as Dr Bowman felt they would be too young to look after themselves. I remember climbing on the branch of a fallen log to get a good view of the erection of their big tents on Willinga. Mrs Bowman, perhaps disconcerted by my stickybeaking but more likely through kindness, came over to ask me if I would like a sweet. The use of the word 'sweet' in this context was quite new, but I was quick to learn. To me, sweets were simply lollies.

The Bowmans were keen beach fisherfolk, using the traditional beach worms for bait. In each generation, the girls were encouraged to learn the tricky art of worming using the fingers only. Janet Arnold (née Bowman) recalled being offered ten shillings for her first worm, but the pay thereafter dropped to a mere shilling per worm.

Figure 38: Rodney Ellis and Charles Parsons with jewfish, Bawley Point, 1934. Rodney was the grandson of the owner of the Bawley Point sawmill.
Source: Bruce Hamon.

THEY CAME TO MURRAMARANG

When Willinga became more crowded, the Bowmans moved their camp to Pretty Beach (then called Island Beach), which they must have had almost to themselves for years. Frank Evans supplied them with water in 200 litre drums, and their heavy camping gear was stored between trips at London's place. Later, the Bowmans returned to Bawley Point, building a cottage in Lorikeet Close, which is still enjoyed by their descendants.

I should be able to write a separate book about local fishing! My father was a keen fisherman, and I have been returning to Bawley mainly for the fishing ever since I lived there. Gut lines first became available in the early '20s. My earliest memories are of cord lines for both beach and rock fishing. The cord lines were rigged with a sinker on the end and one or two hooks on dropper loops above the sinker. The lines favoured for rock fishing were of Irish linen and described as '36-cord'. They were very strong; it was only just possible to break a snagged 36-cord line.

Rock fishing was for snapper, and to a lesser extent for groper. The beaches were fished for bream and whiting. Blackfish (luderick) or tailor were not fished for at all, and I don't think we even suspected the existence of black drummer. Octopus, usually called starfish, was the preferred snapper bait, as it stayed on the hook well, but fish bait was used occasionally. The north-east corner of Bawley and the rather ill-defined gutter due east of the Trig Station were the favoured spots on Bawley Point, but if there was too much sea at those places my father fished the 'Basin', or even from the rocks about 100 metres east of the wharf. The cord lines were flaked out on rock or beach before throwing out. If this was not done carefully the line would tangle. Rods were used by visitors to the area, but were slow to catch on with the locals. Most of my early fishing was from the beaches, using gut lines wound on a bottle. The line could be thrown directly off the end of the bottle, but in playing a fish it was usual to drop the bottle on the sand and let the recovered line fall.

Was the fishing much better then? Here I must be cautious since in this field especially memory plays tricks, and of course no records were kept. For what it's worth, my feeling is that things haven't changed much! Snapper and groper are probably scarcer, and perhaps whiting, but I have certainly had some catches of other species recently that were as good as any, and conversely can remember many fishless sorties in the '20s. Perhaps I've become more skilled with advancing years.

I started school at age seven, at Murramarang. This would have been August 1924, so my first full school year was 1925. I walked the two miles each way, barefooted like the rest. The school had only around 15 students, in six different classes, all in one room and of course with only one teacher. The teachers during my four years there were Mr A. B. Hayes and Mr Brown. Mr Hayes kept in touch with at least one student from those times (Mrs Isabel Vider, née Walker) until his death. I visited him in Sydney in around 1974.

I have only a hazy idea now of the actual schoolwork. Laborious attempts at copying those too beautifully formed copperplate letters in the writing exercise books; 'sums', of course; copying maps; pressing flowers into nature study books. There was little manual work — some attempt at gardening, and folding of squares of brightly coloured paper. We were introduced to chip carving, and I still have a small practice piece from those days, which Mother kept and used for years as a teapot stand. Plasticine was used for modelling. We had slates in the first year or two. Ink in inkwells, stoppered with glass marbles. Those wretched scratchy steel pen nibs, that seemed better designed for the tips of darts than for writing. And singing — aided in some mysterious way by a tuning fork. We were very bashful about singing. I seem to recall that if the teacher didn't continue to lead us, our efforts quickly trailed away to nothing, like a gramophone running down. The school did put on a play called 'Soot and the Fairies'. I was a very unwilling Baron Bootlace, or some such. The play must have taken some organising, as we were an apathetic bunch.

A school inspector (Mr West) came once a year from the Department of Education. Very wrongly, the inspector was portrayed to us as a bogey man, to such effect that on one occasion of an inspector's visit we all scampered off to a nearby patch of she-oaks to hide. I don't recall how we were coaxed back. Another once-a-year event was the gift to every school pupil in the district of a bag of boiled lollies on Empire Day! They were provided and distributed by Blackburns, storekeepers in Milton.

'Rounders' was the most popular game at school. I doubt if I ever saw cricket or football played before going to college in Goulburn. Jacks and marbles were also played, and some ring games such as drop-the-handkerchief.

I suppose these early school days were happy enough. Certainly neither teacher was a tyrant, and there was little in the way of punishment. But we did not like going to school. I suspect this was at least partly an attitude passed on by our parents, whose school years were probably harsher. We used any excuse to stay away from school. The most frequent excuse was rain: either we would get wet and cold (wet weather gear was not so easy to come by) or we might be swept away in flooded creeks. On very wet days, only the teacher would put in an appearance.

Playing truant or 'wagging it' was much talked of, but I'm not sure how many absences from school were a result of truanting. In my case, I had to try it, but once was enough. Olive Hapgood and I decided to raid a patch of watermelons that were growing among maize on Guy's property. We tested a number of melons in the approved way, by cutting out a small triangular piece with a pen-knife. A nice melon was eventually selected, and we ate it and our lunch at the south end of Gannet Beach, then sheepishly made our way home at what we guessed was the right hour.

Soon after I got home there was a phone call from a very agitated Mr Collins (manager of Guy's). He was not so worried about the number of melons we had ruined by our thoughtless testing. But some of the melons we had cut into had been poisoned to deter the rabbits! This was indeed too much, and the sorry truth had to come out. I was made to apologise — a very severe punishment for me. I figured that I was not cut out for a life of crime. Olive, now Mrs Olive Baxter and living at Termeil, remembers the incident, and told me recently she got into trouble that day for being home too early.

Murramarang School closed at the end of 1928, as there were too few pupils. My last two years of primary schooling were at Termeil (1929–30). I rode to school each day on a darling shaggy-coated, cunning little pony named Titch. I suffered many falls from Titch, but came to no real harm, after all, it was not far to the ground. Mr William Peacock was the teacher for these two years. He was a kindly person, and older than either of my former teachers. He saw to it that I applied for a bursary, and promised me a camera if I succeeded. I had that camera for many years.

One return trip from Termeil School caused my parents much anxiety, as I did not get home till about 9 p.m. I was bringing father's suitcase from Termeil, balanced on the pommel of the saddle. This made anything but a walking pace difficult. It had rained heavily all day, so I found the usual crossing of the lake much too deep to tackle. I continued on the north side of the lake to the tramline bridge, but it was under water. I went on then to the mouth of the lake, only to find that the lake had opened to the sea and was much too dangerous to cross. So I rode, still at walking pace, halfway back to Termeil and then took the track around the head of the lake to Murramarang, and thence to Bawley. Of course I enjoyed the adventure; it did not occur to me that anyone might think I had been drowned or swept out to sea!

Opportunities for getting into mischief were rather limited. I remember trying 'tailor-made' cigarettes (father smoked a pipe, or 'rolled his own'), but even these were hard to get. We also smoked candle-bark, pushing smaller pieces into larger ones to get something large enough to stay alight. When electric torches appeared, I found I could catch rabbits at night by running them down while dazzling them in the torch beam. This was harmless enough, but Mrs Hapgood was worried by the flitting lights. Belle Walker and I decided we would give her a bit more to worry about, so prepared some coloured lights whose effect was reinforced by strange yells and howls from both of us while we raced madly over Bawley Point behind her house. Mrs Hapgood came out with a hurricane lantern in one hand — and a rather business-like stock-whip in the other! My senior partner rose to the occasion, admired the stock-whip, 'borrowed' it and cracked it a few times, explaining the while that we were indeed only chasing rabbits. Peace was restored.

Except for campers and guest house clients, very few people came to Bawley Point. One group that made a special impression on me were marine surveyors, who visited Bawley in June 1923 and carried out a water depth survey within about one kilometre of the mill site. This was a great event in such a small and quiet community. Recently, I found a copy of the survey results in the State Archives. Mr H. H. Kelly, the surveyor in charge, was one of the Kelly family who mined shellgrit and made lime at Burrill.[1]

The visit of the marine surveyors would have been my first introduction to marine science, and my only contact with it for many years. Little did I think at the time that I would become a marine scientist, or a scientist of any kind, for that matter.

The survey party set up a crude tide-indicating device attached to the wharf. This had to be read at regular intervals, probably hourly, and the results logged. One of the local lads was given the job. I remember being very curious about this activity. In later years, I have enjoyed working with sets of hourly tide heights, and would have reanalysed these old observations if I had been able to find them.

Another outstanding visitor, almost literally from another world, was Andrew Cunningham, who 'dropped in' by plane, landing his two-seater Gypsy Moth on Juwin Head ('Logpaddock') several times, around 1925. He and his mechanic (Mr Waller?) stayed with us. His plane would have been the first I had ever been close to, and perhaps the first I had seen.

On one visit, he took my father to Sydney and back, while the mechanic stayed at Bawley. Mother and I, and others, were present when they took off. I am sure neither Mother nor I realised that they very nearly didn't make it. They took off towards the east, but were a bit south of the intended track near the crest of the headland. Banking the plane to correct this caused the left wing-tip to touch the ground, leaving a visible furrow several metres long, and some

---

1   McAndrew, A. *Beautiful Burrill*, A. McAndrew, Sydney, 1993, p. 83.

grass on the wing-tip! But father enjoyed the flight, the only one he ever made. They detoured via the spectacular scenery in the upper Clyde valley, west of the Pigeon House.

Andrew had other landing spots near Milton.[2] I do not remember why he chose to land in such a remote spot as Bawley. Perhaps it was the fish? He had a property near Queanbeyan, and was well known in that district for his unorthodox flying. I was sad to learn recently that he was badly injured in a car accident, and took his own life while still in hospital, using a pistol smuggled in by a friend.

The Depression did not worry us very much, or perhaps I was shielded from such troubles. Father was out of work, so the only income was from the paying guests, and the post office, the latter being the only income for months during the winter. I was at school in Goulburn for the worst years. I might not have been able to continue there without the money from the bursary.

My grandmother Mary Reynolds, née Brodie, was born and reared a few kilometres south-west of Milton, but lived most of her life in Sydney, where she married Henry Reynolds. They came to Bawley to live around 1922, after Grandad retired from the Sydney Harbour Trust.

While in Sydney, Gran wrote four novels (*The Heart of the Bush*, *The Selector Girl*, *The Black Silk Stocking* and *Dawn Asper*) and had several short stories and nature articles published in the *Sydney Mail*. I have been told she also wrote *If England Knew*, which was published as a serial in the *Ulladulla and Milton Times*. She wrote under the name of Broda Reynolds. Gran kept writing till she was over 90, as is shown by a poem to celebrate her 93rd year. She did not write other poetry, as far as I know:

> GRATITUDE
> I thank you dear people for this party most rare
> Given me in my ninety-third year.
> And I know you'll repeat it this day twelve months
> If only it happens I'm here.
> There are other fond gestures in memory's chest
> Piled high on a shelf near the door.
> And this I shall place on top of the rest
> With a hope there'll be one or two more.
> For if I could turn backward the swift hand of time
> And live my life over again

---

2   McAndrew, A. *Memoirs of Mollymoke*, A. McAndrew, 1989, pp. 193–8.

I'd begin where I'm leaving off, here among friends
And begin where the narrow track ends.
I'd rake in a lot that I'd wasted in play
Ambition, endeavour and strife,
And blend them with love, for the good of mankind
For it helps in the riddle of life.
I'd pay in a thought or an act every day,
Remembering humanity's need
Then wait for the blossoms and fruit 'twould produce,
For it's strangely like planting a seed.
Or might it not be that I'd make a worse hash
Of the chance given me in this span,
Squandering and wasting the gold dust of time
As only reckless youth can.
It's hard to define at this age-worn hour
Looking back down the dim darkening way,
But why worry o'er space or the years as they count
Life's only a night and a day.
Yet there are just a few words I'd like you to recall
For I say them with fervour and faith,
And you'll hear them again in the sighing of the wind,
There's a life after this for us all.
So away over there on those astral plains
Where the soul is our self-hood alone
I'll be waiting, my friends, mid the sunbeam that blends
With a halo no earthchild has known.
So comrades most true, I'll leave it to you
To remember this day at its fall.
When I murmured good night while the heavens are bright,
And God bless you my friends one and all.

Figure 39: Mary (May or Broda) Reynolds and Henry Reynolds, Bawley Point, c. 1930.
Source: Bruce Hamon.

Although she was a great reader, I do not remember many books in her home at Bawley Point. One might have expected extensive, crammed bookshelves. Perhaps her generosity to friends, even to mere acquaintances, took toll of the stock over the years. This generosity extended to her pets, and she told the tale many times of giving a beautiful piece of fillet steak to the cat, and opening a tin of sardines for herself.

She was a great talker, and was happy in any company as long as she 'held the floor'. Visitors were fascinated, and quickly fell under her spell. She was fond of thumping your arm almost continuously, for emphasis. In later years, she found it hard to continue to dominate the discussion, but would still follow visitors out to the gate, loath to admit tiredness or let them go. But even at the gate, after almost shooing the visitors off, she might single one out and say: 'But not you. I want to talk to you!'

From her parents, Gran had acquired many 'Irishisms'. I can still recall a few. The spellings are mine, and the meanings, well, who knows?: flahulickness; fininst; gosthoon; pig-dog (as an adjective, usually reserved for the weather: 'a pig-dog day').[3]

---

3   The term 'flahulickness' comes from *flaithiúlacht*, meaning generosity. 'Gosthoon' comes from *gossoon*, or *gasúr*, meaning a boy (see Lonergan, D. *Sounds Irish: The Irish Language in Australia*, Lythrum Press, Adelaide, 2004, pp. 54–6, and Margaret Hamon, personal communication) (A.G. and S.F.).

In the Reynolds' first cottage at Bawley, cooking was on a small wood-burning stove. I am fairly sure there was never a recipe book, or a measure other than the very convenient 'handful'. And there would always be an extra handful for the pot. She made jam, especially shaddock, melon and lemon, and blackberry. I recall delicious fried scones, pancakes with lemon juice and sugar, and dumplings. In later years, in what became Johnston's cottage, she used a camp oven to good effect.

Gran took in guests when the guest house business started. I am not sure if this was her own initiative, or a question at least initially of taking an overflow from Mother's place. Some of Gran's guests came back year after year. I recall in particular the Nicholson family from Rose Bay, who came twice a year (Christmas and May) for many years, making the trip in a hire car which then returned to Sydney, returning to Bawley at the end of the holiday to take them home. There was much camping on Willinga Point in those days, and Gran achieved some control over the camping by refusing more than an emergency supply of scarce tank water to those she did not like the look of. They were advised to go on to Kioloa.

Figure 40: Moving two rooms of one of the mill cottages at Bawley Point to a site near the north end of Bawley Point Beach. These rooms became the centre of the cottage lived in by Broda and Henry Reynolds, and presently owned by Pat Johnson. Henry Reynolds (left) and Charlie Clark (bullock driver), c. 1925.
Source: Bruce Hamon.

THEY CAME TO MURRAMARANG

Gran was brought up a Catholic, but at least in later years enjoyed discussions with members of other denominations. She was not above telling a good story about her own minor transgressions. One Good Friday she had a beautiful piece of fillet steak in the meat safe, but felt she should not eat it. But later she admitted to my wife Anne: 'I craved for that fillet steak all day, and in the end I ate it, so as not to lose the respect of my husband.'

To the dismay of some members of the family, she arranged to be buried in the C of E part of the cemetery (to be near her husband), with a Congregational minister officiating (because she liked the fellow), but after a short service in the Roman Catholic church in Milton. That was Gran, indeed.

My grandfather, or 'Dadkins' as my grandmother often called him, was a character in his own right, though always outshone in company by my grandmother. Grandad was a doer, a practical belt-and-braces man who liked nothing more than to potter about in his workshop or garden. He was impatient with those who talked too much. I recall an evening by the fire when a friend and I, and perhaps Gran, discussed religion at some length while Grandad dozed. We were discussing Jesus when Grandad stirred and interjected with two telling words: 'Stump orator!' We gave up after that.

Grandad had an 'Indian' motorcycle. It was not for riding, but for cutting wood. It was jacked up, and bolted to a tree in the yard. A very Heath Robinson rig, involving parts of a sewing machine and a three-bladed homemade fan, was coupled to the rear wheel hub to keep the engine cool. He planned to drive a circular saw via a belt running from the tyreless back wheel. We spent endless hours on this, but seldom got the engine to fire at all, and certainly never got within a cooee of cutting wood. Just as well, as I think the exhaust system was missing. But I learned a lot about petrol engines, specially the mysteries of timing.

His workshop housed a treadle-powered woodturning lathe which he had made while in Sydney. This did not get much use. There was also a home-made and hand-powered vertical drill, which was very effective though rather slow. Grandad was very careful with his tools — after all, the nearest hardware shop was a long way away. He especially treasured the smallest (1/16 inch) twist drill.

Gran and Dadkins kept a cow, and a horse and sulky. They had a garden, which served also as a bank. Doris Stenhouse once offered to dig a few potatoes, but Grandad kept an eye on her, and gave instructions: 'No Doris! Not there! Dig over here!' I wonder if there is still some buried treasure under the present lawns. He kept bees at one stage; I recall him swathed in some kind of netting and collecting a swarm of bees from a low limb down towards the lake. He was a great DIY practitioner and inventor; even to inventing the proverbial new mouse trap. I recall at least two designs that were made, but I do not think they caught anything. Most country people had to 'make do', and Grandad made this almost a religion. He would spend days mending a cheap tin-opener. Some of this rubbed off on me, or was inherited: I often find myself 'doing a Grandad Reynolds job' on some worthless item.

Ralph Johnston stayed with my grandparents after he retired, and looked after them in their old age. When they died (Dadkins in July 1951 and Gran in June 1962) he bought the property, and lived there for the rest of his life, leaving it to his nephew Pat Johnston. Ralph had many pets over the years: wallabies, possums, at least one penguin, cats and dogs. He lavished great care and affection on them, and later in life built a small church in the grounds of the cottage as a memorial to them. This is now a local landmark, and is enshrined in the special language of surfies, who refer to Willinga Point as 'Churchill's'. (They also call it 'Sharky's'.) Before building the church, Ralph had used the local water-worn pebbles, some carried back from as far south as Snake Bay, and pieces of abalone shell, as decorative materials. They were fashioned into architraves in the house, and flower beds in the garden. After a stay in Royal North Shore Hospital, he made dozens of flower vases out of concrete decorated with pebbles and shells; these were given to the hospital. Each Christmas, Ralph bought boxes of 'California' chocolates for most of the residents; I believe these gifts were delivered by wheelbarrow.

Figure 41: Ralph Johnston's memorial to his pets, Johnston Street, Bawley Point.
Source: Margaret Hamon, courtesy of the Johnston family.

Most families had shotguns and rifles, and potted the local wildlife when they could. 'Roos, wallabies, rabbits and duck were the main targets. The 'roos and wallabies were shot for their skins, and were seldom eaten, except for soup made from their tails. The ducks were harder to get, so I have few memories of eating them. 'Gill birds' (red wattle birds) were sometimes shot for a meal, but were not good targets, at least for the poorly maintained pea-rifles used against them.

There was not much interest in the wildlife as such; perhaps there would have been more if there had been books to consult. Koalas should have been in the area, but I did not see any, and do not remember others talking about them. Reg and Innes Collins said they had seen one or two, and Peter Scheele saw one back of Kioloa. He told me there are still some koalas near Benandra. Belle Vider said she saw only one while she lived at Kioloa. It was large, and on the ground, and after some more questioning Belle agreed that yes, it could have been a wombat!

I can think of only a few changes in bird life, but we did no proper birdwatching in the 1920s. The pallid cuckoo, and some honeyeaters, particularly the white-naped, have become less common. The koel, wood ducks, white egrets, and very recently the channel-billed cuckoo, are more common. Galahs, now quite common, did not appear until about 30 years ago. Cattle egrets appeared even more recently.

There was a deposit of peat a few hundred metres west of the lagoon at Murramarang. This started to burn, probably as a result of 'burning off', sometime in the 1920s, while I was going to school at Murramarang. The burning continued for some months, until put out by heavy rain. The 'fire' was really a very slow smouldering, and resulted in gradual death of the grass around the burning area, which I recall as a hole that was eventually a few metres in diameter. Bill Cullen recalled seeing similar burning in the swamp behind Cormorant Beach. About 20 years ago, I mentioned this to a geographer, who was very interested. He had used carbon dating of such deposits in studies of the history of NSW coastal lagoons and lakes. He did not know of the Murramarang deposit.

My grandmother had heard tales about the bodies of Aborigines 'buried' in caves on Durras Mountain, and I remember two attempts we made to find them. At the time, these tales probably came from the Beadman family,[4] who had farmed on the mountain for many years and had only recently left, but there is an earlier reference. In 1870, a travelling reporter of *Town and Country Journal* mentioned it: 'I had heard of a cave, somewhere in the neighbourhood

---

4   See Nicholls, M. 'Do you Remember?', *Ulladulla Times*, 25 July 1990.

of Murrumerang, which had never been explored. It was said to be haunted, and to have entrances both east and west, to be full of stalactites, bats, fossils and other living creatures.' It was said to be 'six miles on our way [south from Murramarang], and 100 yards off it'.[5] He did not find it. This description, at least for the west entrance, fits a small cave on the west side of Durras Mountain, a few hundred metres north of the end of the fire trail that goes up to the mountain from the west.[6]

In our first attempt to find the cave on the east of the mountain, my parents, grandparents and I camped on Durras, in the then recently deserted farmhouse. Getting there was fun: we used a dray or spring cart, drawn by a decrepit splay-footed lop-lipped nag. The route was the old coastal road that climbed the mountain from the north-east. The last rocky pinch near the top was too much for the nag, so we had to carry our food and gear the rest of the way. My father did the searching, but found nothing. Later there was a shorter expedition, this time accompanied by Mr C. W. Peck (author of two volumes of *Australian Legends*), but again with no success. My grandmother thought the caves might have been found and some contents removed by Varney Parkes, son of Sir Henry Parkes, who was living at Conjola around this time.[7]

---

5   *Town and Country Journal*, 26 November 1870.
6   In the 1980s, an Aboriginal elder from the Illawarra area, Mr Dick Henry, told Sue Feary about a huge cave on Durras Mountain that contained Aboriginal skeletal remains wrapped in paperbark and placed on ledges (Feary, S. personal communication) (A.G. and S.F.).
7   McAndrew, A. *Congenial Conjola*, A. McAndrew, 1991, pp. 31–5.

CHAPTER 8
THE 1920S AND 1930S

At Kioloa there have been two families named Moore, though they were not there at the same time.

The earlier family was that of Robert William Stebbings Moore (1885–1951). Robert was born in New Zealand, the third child of Frederick Stebbings Moore, and came to Australia in 1892 with his parents. Frederick worked in the Nelligen sawmill in the late 1890s.

Robert served an apprenticeship in engineering and blacksmithing at Morts Dock, Sydney, then joined H. McKenzie Ltd. In 1908 he was at Kioloa, presumably to set up McKenzie's mill, which started operating a few years later. His wife-to-be, Alice Johnstone, was then at Pebbly Beach, where her stepfather was engineer in the mill. Courting involved a seven-kilometre walk each way. They were married in Sydney in June 1909. Returning to Kioloa, they lived initially on O'Hara's Head, directly above the mill, but later moved to one of the houses in The Avenue. Around 1927 the family moved from Kioloa to Coramba (inland from Coffs Harbour), where Robert Moore set up a new sawmill using machinery salvaged from the Kioloa mill, which had been destroyed by fire. Although their home was at Kioloa for the period 1909–1927, Robert at least had to leave several times to get work, due to the mill closing temporarily.

While living at Kioloa, Robert and Alice Moore had six children. Their fourth child, the late George Moore of Merrylands, NSW, was born in Lakemba in 1915. He recalled travelling from Sydney to Kioloa around 1920 by train and service car. They stayed overnight at Milton, and left the service car at Termeil early the next morning. Mrs Simpson gave them breakfast after which they walked to Kioloa. His father carried him most of the way.[1] The Moores seemed to have enjoyed life at Kioloa. According to George:

> Even though our parents worked long hours, we had picnics of a weekend mainly down to the island [Pretty Beach]. My dad had a hand cart and our provisions and small children were stowed aboard and the adults would pull it through the bush past Snapper Point and the next headland before arriving at the island.
>
> For a time most of our provisions came from Sydney by boat. Groceries from McIlwraths, drapery from Anthony Horderns and Grace Bros' and meat from Sutton Forest. If the ships were delayed our mother would say 'well, what is it going to be for tomorrow?' Bream, whiting, snapper, mutton fish [abalone] or rabbit, whichever was decided on you could bet us boys would bring home the goods.
>
> … The most frequent operation dad had to perform on us was for stone bruises on the soles of the feet. Not wearing shoes the soles of our feet got very tough and thick and the sharp rocks at Kioloa used to cause the damage. The victim was held down while Dad operated with a razor blade; relief was almost instantaneous.
>
> Deep cuts and bleeding were usually treated with Friar's Balsam, and heavy chest colds with Dad's homemade embrocation. Boils etc. were treated with Venice turpentine, or castor oil and Epsom salts.
>
> Apart from fishing, swimming, catching worms [for bait], trapping rabbits, collecting cuttlefish bone [sold, I think, to Michael Anthony], one of our most rewarding ventures was falling a tree with a bee's nest in it. We boys would find the tree and the older ones would fall it. The honey comb was harvested into hessian sugar bags through which the honey would strain out of the comb.
>
> … Virtually all our needs were home made by our parents. Kerosene and candles were our lighting. The kerosene came in four gallon tins packed in pairs in wooden cases. These cases had many uses, such as chairs, cupboards and storage boxes. I have also seen them with rockers nailed on and used as a baby's cradle.
>
> … Our toys were made locally. Dad made our boats and we also had a smoke house for smoking sea mullet when in season. Mum did all our cooking on the open fire or in a camp oven.

---

1 Almost all the information about the Moore family is from an interview with George Moore by H. J. Gibbney, 28 October 1977, and an undated transcript of handwritten reminiscences.

8. THE 1920S AND 1930S

Figure 42: Mill workers' cottages, O'Hara Head, Kioloa, c. 1912.
Source: The Edith and Joy London Foundation of The Australian National University.

George went to school in the small building near Walker's at the top of The Avenue. He also attended Sunday school there, taken by Lily Walker. Their outdoor life made them interested in nature. Foxes were plentiful, and raided fowl houses, usually killing most of the birds. Wire netting was not available, so fowl houses were enclosed by timber. Wallabies and kangaroos were shot and the tails made into soup. Starlings were very plentiful. I like their name 'windtoddles' for what I judge from George's description were red-capped plover ('dotterel' until recently). Mutton bird carcasses were washed up on the beaches virtually every year.

George's father and others built a tennis court, between the south end of the present caravan park and the mill. A dance hall with a beautifully polished floor seems to have been left over from earlier years, as it was being used as a storage shed for feed for the animals. When it was open, George and his mates had great fun sliding along the floor on pieces of bag. Sports meetings were held at Murramarang. These included 'an occasional game of football. We didn't know anything about it, it was half rugby league, half soccer.' The community was almost teetotal, and George could not remember any instances of the locals going to the nearest pub at Termeil. The Moores had big log fires which they sat by in the evenings, talking and dozing till they could not keep awake any longer then hopping into bed to listen to the noises of the sea pounding on the headland.

The young ones invented their own games. A treacle tin full of sand would be fitted with a wire yoke and trundled along the sand as a roller. Toy jinkers were made of cotton reels cut in two, and used to 'play saw mills'. Lengths of scrap timber were stacked and weighted down with stones to make a fort in a little bay (east of the mill site?). This would become a delightful private island as the tide rose, and in calm weather might withstand several tides.

Figure 43: The Avenue, Kioloa, c. 1925.
Source: The Edith and Joy London Foundation of The Australian National University.

George Moore did not remember any Aborigines working or living in the district, nor do I remember any at Bawley Point.[2] There was a part-Aboriginal family named Cooley[3] at Bawley Point when the mill was working, and Grace Jarman remembered an Aboriginal named Billy Page who worked as a mill hand; he was married and had five children. I remember small groups of Aborigines camping overnight on Willinga Point; we saw their camp fires but had no contact with them. Belle and Lily Walker recalled Tom Butler, an American or West Indian

---

2   This seems at odds with Aboriginal oral traditions of widespread employment in the timber industry (A.G. and S.F.).
3   In 1889, the Aborigines Protection Board allocated five acres of land in the Parish of Croobyar, west of Milton to an Aboriginal man, Tom Cooley, who lived in a bark hut and grew vegetables (Goulding and Waters 2005) (A.G. and S.F.).

Negro who was married to an Australian Aborigine. Tom worked for Mr Walker clearing timber, digging wells and doing odd jobs. The Butlers lived down near the mill, and gave their name to Butler's Creek and Butler's Point.[4]

Others living or working at Kioloa about this time were Jack Creer (sawyer), Joe Thompson and Andrew Hogg (saw doctors), Bob Small and later Bert Swan (mill managers), George Mitchell, the Kellond family, who had moved from Bawley Point after the 1922 fire, the Hapgoods, Jack Bevan, Robinson, Backhouse. Small was described as 'a tall well-built sort of fellow; they used to call him the silent one. He wouldn't say two words unless he had to. He was treated with a lot of respect, and was a pretty strict severe sort of fellow.' Bert Swan, who had been in the war, had come from Sydney to open the new mill McKenzie had built, presumably after the fire. He was described as 'stout and not very tall'. George Moore recalled that Swan broke a kneecap while rock fishing with George's dad; he had to be carried back to the mill, and eventually taken to Milton, doubtless a very painful experience.

The second Moore family were relatives of the Londons, and came with them to Kioloa in 1929, when Mrs London bought the property from William Walker. The combined family consisted of Mr Edward Moore and his wife Kate, their three children, Edith (Mrs London), Bernice ('Bobbie') and Humbert, and Mrs London's two children, Joy and Arthur ('Roy'). The family were English, and Mr and Mrs London had been in West Africa till around 1920, when Mr London died there. Humbert Moore had been in Rhodesia. He brought a friend, Walter ('Sonny') Hillier, from England, who was with the family at Kioloa till World War II started. After a period at Cranbrook School in Sydney, Roy went to live at East Lynne, where he worked in an apple orchard. He went from there to live permanently in Sydney.

Mrs London had intended to settle in New Zealand, and some of their furniture was shipped to New Zealand. The family however was stranded in Sydney by a shipping strike, and decided not to go on to New Zealand when the strike ended. They lived in Sydney for a couple of years, then moved to Braidwood where they started to build on Araluen Mountain. But when Joy's grandfather, Edward Moore, became ill in England in 1925, they all returned to England, where they stayed for three years. After nursing Mr Moore back to health they came back to Australia, bringing Joy's grandparents with them.

After another period of living in Sydney they felt an urge to leave the city. While in a bank in Braidwood, Mrs London heard of the Kioloa property. She looked at it, 'fell in love with the place and bought it'. The Moores moved

---

4   Sonny Butler, an Aboriginal fisherman mentioned earlier, is most likely related to Tom Butler (A.G. and S.F.).

in in March 1929; Mrs London and Joy came a few months later. It has been the family home since then. Although the property was in Mrs London's name, it was always referred to as 'Moore's'. Mr Moore did not like the idea of living in a house owned by his daughter, so he bought the house and two acres around it separately.

Figure 44: Joy London's house, Kioloa, c. 1950.
Source: The Edith and Joy London Foundation of The Australian National University.

An early priority after moving in was to enlarge the house, which had only four rooms. This took some time, as they did it themselves: Hum Moore was a good carpenter and engineer, and Sonny Hillier a gifted woodworker. Some rails from the recently abandoned tramlines were used as flooring joists. They mixed their own paint, and made a floor varnish by dissolving old gramophone records in methylated spirit, the colour being controlled by choosing red, brown or black records. Some of the windows of the wrecked *Northern Firth* were used to enclose the south-east corner of the verandah. They also worked hard to improve local roads (see Chapter 6).

As powered farm machinery was scarce, much use was made of a seven-seater Hudson Model M car, which was the only car in the district during their early years. The car was nicknamed 'The Ambulance' as it was used for all emergencies. According to Joy London: 'we did everything with that old thing. We ploughed with it and we hauled stringers with it to make some of the bridges. It was last seen carting shellgrit from Cronulla about 1936 after we sold it.'[5]

---

5   *Australian National University News*, Vol. 10, No. 1, May 1975, p. 9.

Home life was simple. Hum Moore made his own radios, and the family shared in this novel form of entertainment when the static permitted. They made soap; some of it from tallow salvaged from the *Northern Firth*. Wine was made from grapes, blackberries and other fruits. Mrs London also made liqueurs based on gin. It was Joy's job to make the soft drinks. Reading, knitting and crochet occupied the hours between their 6.30 p.m. dinner and 9 p.m. supper.

Figure 45: Hum Moore and the 32-volt property generator, 1947.
Source: The Edith and Joy London Foundation of The Australian National University.

Joy London has fond memories of her mother, who always wanted to preserve the property as far as possible in its native state. Her mother encouraged the family to 'pull together and make this a good place, a happy worthwhile place'. Mrs London dispensed first aid, organised social gatherings, and had a tennis court built by local volunteers. Joy said:

> Mum was a very quiet type of person. She was placid and could always see the two sides of every question. You could never get her riled, but you knew when she was angry: she'd just take one look at you and you would know. She was a great needle and crochet worker and loved reading, particularly books on Egyptian archaeology. She'd also read every *National Geographic* magazine from cover to cover. She'd always say: 'Cast the small things out of your minds: the day-to-day things.'

I can recall my parents' slight suspicion of the new settlers at Kioloa, expressed in comments like 'why on earth would they want to make a road *there*?' Such an attitude seems strange, but I suppose it was a common small-town reaction to anything new.

Setting out full details of the ownership of land becomes difficult and tedious after around 1930, so only a brief account will be attempted. The Kioloa property (blocks E, G, H, see Map 1) remained in the name of Mrs McKenzie until transferred to Walker in 1928 for a nominal sum (see Chapter 5); it was then sold to Mrs London in 1929. It remained with the Londons till 1975, when Joy London gave block E to The Australian National University: we will return to this in Chapter 9.

Figure 46: Joy London with Bimbo.
Source: The Edith and Joy London Foundation of The Australian National University.

Block D ('Bundle' or 'Bundle Hills') was owned by Frank Guy, 1916–27, then by Teddy Wyld who ran a few head of cattle on it. The soil was poor, and he did no good on it, eventually going broke. He did not have a house on the property, but lived in one of The Avenue cottages at Kioloa. Ownership then passed in turn to the Rural Bank, Robert Douglas Hassell, Charles Allan Penny and Joseph Dudley Swanston, Noel William Johnson, and Ronald James Bray. Bray cut the millable timber off it. It was then partly subdivided by Willmore and Randell. The unsubdivided part was bought by John Wallace Alford, then O. and L. Froude.

Blocks B and C, which together were the 'Murramarang' block inherited by Evan Evans III in 1906 and run after Evan's death by Alf Evans (see Chapter 3), were acquired in 1917 by Lindsay Wilson. He was described as 'a very bossy man; well educated but impractical'. He did little with the land. He donated the one-acre block for Murramarang School, which was built around 1922. At the time of his death in the 1940s he was living a lonely life in a bush hut between Milton and Ulladulla.

Wilson sold block C, on which Murramarang House stands, to Billy Orr in 1928. Orr's correct surname was Scott-Orr; this name was used by his brother, who was the doctor in Milton at about that time, but Billy preferred the simpler version. He had been to Sydney University to study economics or law, but I do not think he completed the course. He just did not like the city. He went jackarooing on a sheep station, liked the life and decided to buy a place of his own. He bought block C at Murramarang, but lived in the small dairy (or cheese factory?) about 100 metres south of the main house. I remember visiting him there; he had a large open fireplace and facing it was a large deep armchair, where he must have spent many a comfortable but lonely hour. His idea of heaven was a place where it was always time to get up, but you knew you did not have to! He ran about 300 sheep on the property; according to Neil Evans the sheep did fairly well after they found the best time of year for drenching. Orr enlisted as a private when war broke out, and was the first from the district to be killed in the war. He was killed in Syria, and buried at Damascus.

Neil Evans rented Murramarang from Orr in 1939, and stayed there till 1946. Orr had been engaged to Belle Walker, but after this was broken off he became friendly with Marie Kellond, to whom he left the property when he joined up. Marie sold it to Hassell at the low price of £700.

Several families lived in Murramarang House while Billy Orr owned it, but I am not sure of all their names or lengths of stay; I recall only Kellond, Donovan and Bevan. Mrs Bevan said Billy Orr had asked her to start a guest house there, with furniture from Orr's mother's home at Bowral, but there was not sufficient furniture and the scheme did not go ahead.

Block A, 'Willinga', remained in the Guy family after Frank Guy's death in 1931 (he was injured when opening or closing a gate while on horseback, and died of tetanus). It was later subdivided (see Chapter 9).

Bawley Point Guest House moved in 1932 from 'the old home' near the mill site to its present location in Johnston Street, where the Cullen family had lived till the mill fire. The move must have been a bold venture for my parents; perhaps they were already committed before the Depression reached its worst phase. They designed the place, and my father built it with help from Frank Carriage and probably others. Mother spent many anxious hours worrying over the design: how many rooms? Floor plan details? How large? And so on. I am not sure how it was financed; we would not have had much reserve capital.

As originally built, the guest house contained five bedrooms, a bathroom (with one of those wretched temperamental chip heaters which startled guests with its woof! woof! woof!), a lounge/dining room, kitchen, post office, and two rooms for my parents at the back. At the same time, or very soon after, an additional three rooms were added in a separate building, called the 'aeries'. Within a few years, electric light from a 32-volt battery with petrol-driven charging generator was added. Ralph Johnston was very helpful at the time, and enthusiastic about the whole project. He thought up a name for the house, 'Brulema', ingeniously fashioned from the Hamons' given names: Bruce, Les and Alma. He had a bronze nameplate cast; this was near the front door for decades. In recent times the front aspect of the place has been dominated by two very large pine trees. My grandmother bought these at Paddy's Market in Sydney, as tiny seedlings in jam tins, for 18 pence each. They provided daytime roosts and nesting sites for a colony of Rufous Night-Herons (Nankeen Night-Herons) for many years.

Figure 47: 'New' guest house, Bawley Point, mid-to-late 1930s.
Source: Bruce Hamon.

My parents left the guest house in around 1939, building a new house to replace the one Kellonds had lived in. I think the guesthouse was leased for a time, and that my mother took it over again, but it was sold after a few years. Mrs Bailey, Mr and Mrs Fred Bucholtz, and Mr and Mrs Bill Fuller owned it at various times. The present owners, Peter and Robin Cormack, have developed the restaurant side of the business, as well as acquiring the adjoining property to the south to increase the accommodation.[6]

Figure 48: Bawley Point Guest House before its closure in 2001.
Source: Margaret Hamon.

My parents moved briefly to Duckmaloi and Grenfell, where Father worked for Mr Gerald Haskins, a consulting engineer who had stayed in the guest house several times. Later they retired to Mollymook, where Father died in 1958 and Mother in 1976.

The Kellond family have had a long association with the area. Billy Kellond was blacksmith at Bawley Point mill from around 1912, and four of the seven girls in the family were born at Bawley Point, Mrs Backhouse from Termeil being the midwife. According to Grace Kellond (now Mrs Ray Jarman) they lived first in a house 'right on top of Bawley Point', but later moved to a delightfully situated cottage near the north end of the beach, where the Settree family had lived while the *Douglas Mawson* was being built. Grace started school in the temporary schoolroom on the north side of Willinga Lake around 1920, and remembers hating it: she 'howled all the way'. Later she went to Murramarang

---

6   This information was current at the time of the book's first publication in 1994. The house closed in 2001 and is now a private residence (A.G. and S.F.).

School. After leaving school, she returned for a while to do a correspondence course, mainly to bolster the enrolment numbers so the school would not close. The Kellonds moved to Termeil after the mill fire at Bawley Point. While the family were living there, Billy Kellond worked at Brooman. They moved then to Kioloa, where they lived in one of The Avenue cottages. After the Kioloa mill closed, Billy Kellond worked at Pebbly Beach. Grace remembers walking with her sister Marie from Kioloa to Pebbly Beach and back in a day, to take supplies to her father when he did not come home for the weekend. The family was living in Murramarang House at the time of the *Northern Firth* wreck (1932). Mr Kellond was working for Billy Orr at that time; one of his duties was repair work on Murramarang House.

My father told the following tale about Billy Kellond. Billy was good at catching beach worms for bait. It was often his practice to throw each worm up the beach instead of putting it in a tin attached to his belt. After one difficult worming session on North Beach, he found to his horror that the seagulls had gobbled all the worms. He went home, got his shotgun and dealt severely with the seagulls. I have often pondered this story, as no wormer in his right mind would throw worms up the beach these days; perhaps on that fateful day the gulls had only just developed a taste for worms? Incidentally, Billy Kellond, and no doubt other blacksmiths, made the iron worming pliers that were fashionable at the time. Their jaws were wound with a few layers of knitting wool.

Figure 49: From left: Gwen Kellond, Pat Kellond (in front of Gwen), Bobbie Moore, Mrs George Moore, Marie Kellond, Clarrie Kellond. Kioloa Beach, c. 1925. Note the sparse timber cover on O'Hara Head.
Source: R. A. Moore, Depot Beach, NSW.

Paul Vider was manager of the mill at Bawley Point, starting in 1912 or perhaps earlier. Paul's father had been in the French Navy, and deserted his ship in Sydney by jumping overboard and swimming ashore with a few belongings. He married and settled in Braidwood, where he ran several not very successful ventures. One of these was a sawmill near Nelligen at a place still called 'Vider Town'. Paul got his first job in the milling industry in Bellingen, and was transferred from there to Bawley Point. Their youngest child, Marie (Mrs Clarence Rogerson of Ulladulla) was born at Bawley Point. The family moved to a farm in Milton probably around 1920, and from there to Bombala in 1922.

The Brownes lived at Bawley Point from around 1910 to 1920. Henry Browne was a saw doctor, but also worked on the main saw bench and drove the horse teams which pulled logs on the tramline. Initially they lived in one of the cottages near the mill, but moved later to a cottage on the north side of Willinga Lake. Their eldest child Heather, now Mrs Sharp, remembers there were only three buildings on the north side of the lake: their cottage and the stables on the eastern side of the tramline, and one other house on the western side, near the lake. This house was built high above the ground as a precaution against flooding. One room of this house was used for some time as a schoolroom.

Heather remembers particularly the birth of her brother Bob while they were living at Willinga. She and other young children were sent with her father that day for a ride on the timber bogies. They came back to the mill at midday and were given lunch by Mrs Davenport, who said: 'I've got some news for you; since you left home this morning your mother has found a little baby brother for you.' Heather must have asked for details, and was told: 'Oh, she was getting water from the well, and the little baby was pumped up with the water.' Heather could not wait to get home, where she spent much time and energy at the pump, to see if she too could 'pump up a baby'. Her leg slipped between two boards covering the well, giving her a nasty graze on the shin, which left a still-visible mark.

A sadder story concerned their dog. There was a lot of thick tea tree and scrub about, so the dog had to be anointed with mineral turps to kill ticks. Unfortunately, Heather came too close with a naked light and the poor dog caught fire. He took off from the house like a rocket, heading as they believed towards the lake to douse the flames. Searching proved fruitless, and they were resigned to his tragic loss, when a fortnight later he returned, minus half of each ear and part of his tail. They nursed him back to health, and had him around for many years.

Heather remembered the horse teams. When shown a photo of a team pulling logs across the tramline bridge, she exclaimed: 'Oh! That must be old Prince, that white horse in the lead!' She also has vivid but unpleasant memories of

THEY CAME TO MURRAMARANG

Murramarang lagoon, which was portrayed as 'haunted' and 'bottomless', no doubt to prevent tragedies when children strayed there after school. George Moore and I also remembered being told that the lagoon was bottomless.

Not many aircraft have been towed out of trouble by a bullock team, but this happened at Murramarang around 1939. Neil Evans recalled that there were bush fires about, and the smoke was thick. Neil and his brother Windsor and another man were fishing on Murramarang beach when a plane flew over, very low. The pilot dropped a note wrapped in a glove. This landed in the water, so the note was unreadable. A second note was dropped, and read: 'Is the sand soft or hard?' An answer was written in the sand and the plane landed on the beach, but when it stopped the wheels sank in the sand. Neil went home to Murramarang, harnessed his team of bullocks and pulled the plane up to the flats behind the beach, then to where Harrington Crescent is now and on to the north end of Gannet Beach.

The plane was owned by Adastra Airlines, and had on its fuselage 'Fly with Adastra'. It was on its way to Merimbula, but was low on fuel. Neil drove the pilot and passenger to Milton where they stayed overnight. Andy Clugston from the garage brought the pilot and passenger back the following day, with standard petrol for the plane. The plane took off towards the west, about where Rosemary Avenue is now.

Later, in the 1950s, another aircraft visited the area, landing on Bawley Point. It was a light plane piloted by Artie Herne, who had grown up at Termeil. Margaret Hamon remembers the plane landing, and being tied up to the tea tree bushes which covered much of the presently settled area of the Point; there was too little soil for the tent pegs usually used to make a small plane secure.

Human skeletons and artefacts were found at Murramarang in the 1920s, in at least two different places. The first find was made by Reg and Innes Collins around 1920, in the sand dunes near the north end of Murramarang Beach. The sands had been shifted by the wind, to reveal a skeleton and crescent-shaped copper plate, which bore the following inscription:

WOONDU

Of Amity Point

REWARDED BY THE GOVERNOR

FOR THE ASSISTANCE HE AFFORDED, WITH FIVE OF HIS COUNTRYMEN

TO THE SURVIVORS OF THE WRECK OF THE STEAMER 'SOVEREIGN'

BY RESCUING THEM FROM THE SURF OF MORETON ISLAND

ON 11th MARCH 1847

ON WHICH MELANCHOLY OCCASION 46 PERSONS WERE DROWNED

AND BY THE AID OF THE NATIVES 10 WERE SAVED

Amity Point is at the north end of North Stradbroke Island, Queensland, and is separated from the southern tip of Moreton Island by the narrow and dangerous South Passage. *The Sovereign*, a wooden paddle boat of 119 tons, was en route from Brisbane to Sydney, and attempting a shortcut through South Passage. My grandmother, Broda Reynolds, must have been visiting us soon after the find, and published a note about it.[7] The note was seen by Brisbane historian Thomas Welsby, who contacted the Collins family and acquired the brass plate. It is now in the hands of the Royal Historical Society of Queensland. Welsby wrote at some length about the wreck.[8] He knew two of the six Aborigines involved in the rescue, one of whom still had his brass plate in the early 1880s. This plate has since disappeared, and the other four have never been seen, so the Woondu plate is the only one whose whereabouts is known. Similar plates, called king plates, breastplates or gorgets, were often given to Aborigines as rewards.

At the time the Woondu plate was found, it was assumed the skeleton found with it was that of Woondu, but Welsby thinks this unlikely. He points out that it would be very unusual for an Aborigine to travel alone so far through lands controlled by hostile tribes. A more likely explanation, in his view, is that the plate was bartered, and may have passed through several hands on its way to Murramarang. The skeleton was given decent burial by the Collins boys, and the grave outlined with shells and stones.

The site of the second find of human remains was on Murramarang headland, about 100 metres west of the north end of Cat and Kitten Beach (the small beach opposite Brush Island). Belle Vider (née Walker) and her friend Margaret Collins were riding in the area when they noticed the corner of a box protruding from the sand. Here is Belle's description:

> I discovered the edge of a box, just see it in the sand, and I said to my girlfriend 'this might be a hidden treasure, let's dig it out'. So we started digging and got a shock because we came to hair, human hair, and we kept going and I suppose we were pretty game and we unearthed a skull, and there was a hole right in the middle of the forehead. Anyway, I dug further down and I could see whoever it was had been buried in a material, it was a twill material, it was green, a very dark green, whether that had been the change of colour over the years I don't know. At the feet the person had a pair of boots, you could tell what they were — decayed — but they were boots, and the complete skeleton was wrapped in a blanket. I pulled little bits of it out and I could tell it was a blanket. Well we covered that over and kept walking, then I found the rim of a billycan and I pulled it up and it all fell to pieces, so we dug in it, and out of the billycan I found an old penny, King George, I think it might have been [King George] III. It was bigger than our other pennies.

---

7 *The Sydney Mail*, 3 November 1920.
8 Thompson, A. K. *The Collected Works of Thomas Welsby*, Jacaranda Press, Brisbane, 1967, Vol. 2, pp. 87–92. A photo of the plate faces, p. 168.

THEY CAME TO MURRAMARANG

And there were two badges, two cricketer's badges, one had a cricketer standing each side of an Australian coat of arms, which I was told must have been the first Australian coat of arms. They must have changed it. And underneath — one cricketer had a bat and the other cricketer had a ball in his hand — and underneath was 'Advance Australia'. After we sort of cleaned them up, polished them and they were brass, and with that buckle there was another buckle, and that just had a bat ball and stumps. Well, we found the penny, we found the badges, we found an old cutthroat razor, we found a knife, spoon and fork which we could tell what they were, and we found a tin matchbox, not a wooden matchbox, of tin, but the same size as a safety matchbox, nothing in it, and I can't remember what else, but we decided we would share everything up, so my girlfriend took the penny and I took the badges. There was a comb — it seemed to be a person's personal belongings. So we dug under that can and there was another skeleton. I never dug completely round it except I knew there was a skull underneath. We just covered it all over again. Well we shared up the loot and I took mine and my mother was so upset about it she shot them out and said the person could have died of a disease and they'd buried everything but I found them and I polished them and I got them pretty good, so I could read 'Advance Australia' on the buckle. They were like belt buckles, I'm sure that's what they were, but over the years moving from Kioloa and from one place to another I've just lost trace of them.

Later, when Belle was working at the Bawley Point guest house, she took anthropologists from the Australian Museum to the site. Belle said they found that 'somebody had been there and unearthed the whole skeleton. I found everything bar the skull, most of the bones, and they [museum people] were disappointed because they wanted to identify them, whether they were Aboriginal or a white person.' The museum people were also interested in the stone implements and shells at the site, which proved to be an extensive Aboriginal midden.[9]

The human remains were in a small part of the area covered by the midden. At least five skeletons were eventually found. My grandfather had some of the skulls on a shelf in his workshop, behind a wooden partition which he would slide back with a flourish when he wanted to startle visitors. Later he destroyed the skulls.

I remember seeing some of the skulls and human bones on the sandhills site. I saw also a few buttons, and I think some clothing and a buckle, and the metal end of a gun cartridge of early design. It had a firing pin protruding from the

---

9   This may be a reference to the early 1970s, when a geomorphologist from the University of Sydney did some auger holes and test excavations to determine the stratigraphy of the site, which proved difficult due to extensive dune erosion from grazing and vehicles (Hughes, P. Murramarang. A report on fieldwork at this site in November–December 1972 and some preliminary findings, unpublished student report, University of New South Wales, School of Geography, 1973) (A.G. and S.F.).

side, and I have been told it was called a 'pin-fire' cartridge and would date from about the 1860s. Some, but not all, of the skulls were Aboriginal, according to the anthropologists.

Marie McClung (née Kellond) remembers when the skeletons were found. She fossicked around the area once while her father was fishing off the rocks below, and found a gold ring, which she took down proudly to show him. His reaction, from superstition or a fear of disease, was that the ring should be got rid of without delay, so Marie threw it into the sea. Marie made some other finds at a different site, described as on the hill south-west of Murramarang lagoon. One item found there was an 1813 threepenny piece. Mrs Neil Mison (née Gladys Cullen), who grew up at Bawley Point, is reported as saying:

> Saturday afternoon 'fun' for boys and girls was to collect together on the sandhills, where the chief game was to 'make a man'. This consisted of digging into the sandhills for bones of human beings, which were not hard to find ... the game was that children sought to complete a full skeleton, and the first one to achieve this won the game.[10]

Most of these finds have never been explained. The stone implements present no problem, as they are part of the Aboriginal midden, but what are we to make of the others?[11] Perhaps the part of the midden where human remains were found was used as a local cemetery in the early decades of settlement. No other cemetery area was mentioned in the papers I have seen. The numerous bones implied in the above account by Gladys Cullen would be consistent with the cemetery idea. Belle Vider said her mother had told her that a child of one of the Evanses had been buried 'at Wilford's Point [Murramarang headland] before 1910'; this suggests that the area was used as a cemetery.

In more recent times, three people were buried in the Bawley Point/Kioloa area. Pross Andrews, who was killed while timber-getting before 1910, is believed to be buried in the gully that bears his name, north-west of The Avenue at Kioloa. Jack Bennett was buried in the sand hills opposite The Avenue at Kioloa, around 1910. Bennett was an old man, employed by Mr Walker to do odd jobs. He died when a dray-load of posts capsized on him. At Bawley Point there was a lone grave, fenced and with lilies growing on it, a few hundred metres north of the present shop. Heather Sharp (née Browne) told me it was the grave of Gordon Switzer (or Switzki), aged around six, who died around 1916. Heather was present at the funeral. The boy's parents were German, and 'kept to themselves' in a cottage on Bawley Point, which was separate from the mill cottages. Neil

---

10 Nicholls, M. *Ulladulla Times*, 25 July 1990.
11 Several partial skeletons, identified by archaeologists as being Aboriginal, have been accidently uncovered on Murramarang headland over the decades. Some were held by NPWS and others were at universities, but all have now been repatriated back into the midden (A.G. and S.F.).

Evans claimed there were around 40 Aboriginal graves outlined with stones near or on the sandhills 'about the middle of Murramarang beach'. I do not know what to make of this claim. Such a large burial area would surely have been well known, but no one else has mentioned it.

Walter Scott was the mailman between Kioloa, Bawley Point and Termeil in the 1920s, and probably much earlier. He lived in a shack about one kilometre inland from Merry Beach. The place was untidy to say the least, as was Walter himself, with his uncombed hair and beard and slovenly attire. He grew a few fruits and vegetables, but we were warned not to accept anything from him if we made a rare visit. He had about 20 cats, which kept him warm at nights. When my mother inquired about one cat which had been sick, Walter said that when he woke up he found the 'thunderin' cat dead around my neck'. Belle Vider recalled that her mother kept a special spoon and cup for Walter's use. Mrs Walker took pity on Walter one Christmas and gave him Christmas dinner. She would not invite him into the house, but set up for him in the post office. When he had finished 'there were bones all over the place'. Joy London recalled Walter's honesty: he would always pay next visit for a COD parcel, if he was not carrying the required amount of cash.

Walter married late in life, but it was too much for him — he died within a year or two. He had advertised, or answered an advertisement, for a wife. Two women came at least to Termeil, looked at Walter, then went back. Later, somewhat spruced up by well-wishers, he went to Sydney to meet a woman who had come over from Adelaide. They married and came back to Kioloa to live. After Walter's death, Mrs Scott stayed at Kioloa, where she taught at the school for several years. Although she was always known as 'Mrs Scott', Walter's account of the marriage throws some doubt on its legality. Joy London said Walter told her 'there was this service going on in the church so we just went in'.[12] Asked if he had gone before a minister he replied: 'Oh no, when we came we just put some money in the box and that was that'.

After Walter Scott, the important mail link to Termeil was kept going by Frank Evans till he retired in 1944, then by Windsor Evans. Windsor also delivered milk in the district for some years from the dairy herd on Moore's at Kioloa.

---

12 *Australian National University News*, Vol. 10, No. 1, May 1975, p. 10.

8. THE 1920S AND 1930S

Figure 50: Walter Scott, mailman, Kioloa–Termeil, c. 1930.
Source: The Edith and Joy London Foundation of The Australian National University.

Figure 51: Bawley Point Beach, c. 1934
Source: Bruce Hamon.

The Electoral Roll for 1922 lists several names for Kioloa and Bawley Point, in addition to those already mentioned.[13] For Kioloa the names are Hadley, Holmes, Levien, Tiernan, Woods. The same reference lists the following for Bawley Point: Bonner, Byrne, Cork, Davenport, Jarman, Johnson, Killmore, Lee, Rose, Thompson. I do not remember even a mention of some of these. Eric Simpson remembered some of them: Bonner was an elderly single man who had come from Sydney, and worked as a mill hand; Tom Lee was also elderly and had four or five sons who were mill workers, while Mrs Lee operated a boarding house, or at least provided meals; Byrne had the mail run Termeil to Kioloa, and died as the result of a sulky accident; Hadley was a mill hand with a glass eye, who was responsible for an injury to Eric's finger; Tiernan was tallish and single; Ernie (Edward in the electoral roll) Jarman was mill boss. The following were living at Termeil, but were in the timber industry: James Backhouse (bush foreman); James Backhouse junior (teamster); Charles Beileiter (mill hand); John Bevan (timber cutter); William Boag (teamster); George Shoebridge (timber cutter); Albert Smith (timber cutter). It is hard to know what to make of the electoral

---

13 Reynolds, G. *Milton District Electoral Roll 1922*, Possum Printing, Batemans Bay, 1992, p. 84.

rolls. Although it was compulsory to register and vote, many in such remote places did not bother, and those who did were often tardy in notifying change of address after the frequent moves forced on them.

World War II came at the close of this period. With improved communications and a threat of invasion, the small local community was not as isolated from events as it was in World War I. Both mills were out of action for several years before the war, and the tourist industry had only barely started, so there were few people about. Billy Orr, Keith Simpson of Termeil, and Sonny Hillier and Bill Bevan of Kioloa enlisted. Some joined the Volunteer Defence Corps. My father was in the VDC on coast watching duties, stationed at Bendalong. I think he also worked for part of the time building boats at Ulladulla.

The cottages in The Avenue at Kioloa were taken over by around 30 army personnel for part of the war, when preparations were being made to resist a possible invasion. Road signs were removed. Joy London recalls that they were required to report any planes or shipping to Sydney, and that they had a direct phone line for this, and a special code which was changed daily. She also recalled that the army men in the cottages went wild at times, driving at speed and shooting kangaroos from their vehicles. One of their number was thrown from a vehicle and killed.

Figure 52: Old crane mill at Bawley Point. This picture was taken around 1950, almost 30 years after the mill was destroyed.
Source: Bruce Hamon.

CHAPTER 9
RECENT DEVELOPMENTS[1]

A very important event in the area in recent years was undoubtedly Joy London's gift of 860 acres at Kioloa to The Australian National University. The deeds of this land, the 'Home Block' (block E on Map 1), were handed over on 1 March 1975, and the property then became known as the Edith and Joy London Foundation. This generous gift was Joy's way of honouring her mother, and particularly her mother's wish that the property be preserved as nearly as possible in its present state instead of following the usual path of subdivision.[2] The property had been the home of the Moore and London family since 1929 — about half the time since it was granted to Carr in 1842. The family had worked hard there; it was happy work, and they had loved the place.

The property had been left to Joy after her mother's death in November 1958. Joy's grandparents Edward and Kate Moore had died in 1933 and 1942 respectively, so only Joy and her aunt and uncle were left to run the property. With no close relatives, it was time to think hard about the eventual fate of the property. It was originally offered in turn to some charities, but they declined. This might seem strange: the main difficulty they saw was that of guaranteeing to maintain the character of the property 'in perpetuity'. Then Joy, who had become friendly with Pat Walker, wife of Professor Don Walker of ANU, asked Pat casually if ANU might be interested? They were indeed.

---

1   This chapter was the last in the first edition of the book. When the present tense is used in this chapter, it refers to circumstances in 1993. This helps to retain some of the speculative nature of the chapter. An updated reflection on Murramarang at the time of the publication of this second edition is presented in the following epilogue to this book (A.G. and S.F.).
2   *Australian National University News*, Vol. 10, No. 1, May 1975.

■ THEY CAME TO MURRAMARANG

A property of this size and diversity provides many opportunities for university staff and students to carry out carefully planned field projects that might run for long periods — decades, or even centuries. It also satisfies many shorter-term requirements, such as giving students first-hand experience of gathering data under field conditions.

The foundation property is run by a management committee. Joy London is a member of this committee, and in this way continues an active interest in the foundation. She continues to live in the main homestead at the top of The Avenue. With the help of the late Neil Evans, she ran the farming side for the foundation in its early years.

Another important event has been the gazetting of Murramarang National Park in May 1973. This park extends from Pretty Beach to Batemans Bay, and includes some areas that were previously privately owned, such as the land on Durras Mountain. The National Parks and Wildlife Service also administers the Murramarang Aboriginal Area, which includes the extensive midden referred to earlier. Setting up the park was the culmination of many years of investigation and planning by NPWS staff and by private groups, including the National Parks Association.

For the rest of the area, the period since World War II has been one of continued growth, and improvement in facilities. The number of houses rose slowly at first, to only 72 in 1964, but then increased more rapidly to 220 in 1977 and an estimated 650 in 1993.[3] About one third is permanently occupied, so there are enough residents to support local shops and tradespeople.

The concrete bridge over Willinga Lake was opened in April 1969, and the road from Kioloa through Bawley Point to the Princes Highway was sealed within the next decade. For the first time, residents and visitors could rely on access in any weather, except the rare occasions when the lake was high enough to flood the bridge approaches. Electric power lines were put through a few years earlier, around 1966, and the navigation light on Brush Island was installed in 1967. A school bus service from Kioloa and Bawley Point to Ulladulla started around 1971. In 1993 this service catered for nearly 100 pupils. The Education Department is considering a re-introduction of the local school scheme, and is looking for a suitable site.

---

3   *Bawley Point–Kioloa: Planning Issues and Policies,* Shoalhaven City Council, Planning Department, 1992, p. 35.

9. RECENT DEVELOPMENTS

Figure 53: Transfer of title to the Edith and Joy London Foundation property from Miss Joy London to The Australian National University, 1 March 1975.
From left: Professor D. N. F. Dunbar (acting Vice-Chancellor, ANU), Mr Pat Johnston (Miss London's accountant), Mr Bill Duke (Miss London's legal advisor), Miss Joy London.
Source: The Edith and Joy London Foundation of The Australian National University.

The earliest substantial development in the area was at Bawley Point, where around 50 quarter-acre (0.1 ha) blocks were surveyed from Crown Land south of the guest house in the 1940s. This was followed by Alan Guy's subdivision of part of the Willinga property around 1962, which had been left to him and his brother Jack by their grandfather Francis Harrington Guy. Their father, Francis Augustus Guy (1891–1927), had died before their grandfather. This was the area on Juwin headland, and behind Gannet Beach. I was present when these blocks were auctioned, and can remember the mutterings of gloom when only one block was sold. The further subdivision of the eastern part of 'Willinga', on the headland at the south end of Gannet Beach, and on the west of Murramarang Road, was carried out in stages and over a period of years.

Other early subdivisions were at Kioloa, opposite the camping area, at Merry Beach and on Bawley Point. Subdivisions on the west side of Murramarang Road have generally been later, and the block sizes larger. The first part of the Voyager Crescent subdivision was around 1973, and the large size of the blocks here and elsewhere was due to terrain and poor absorptive capacity of the soil. A historically important subdivision was made in 1981, when the home block for Murramarang House was reduced to 10 acres. It was bought at that time by Mrs le Febvre (now Mrs Truter), who plans to live in the old house in a few years' time.

Figure 54: Entrance to the Edith and Joy London Foundation, The Australian National University, Kioloa, before the renovation of the cottages on The Avenue.
Source: Margaret Hamon.

The small shop on Bawley Point was started by Bruce Brown in 1972. The Bawley Point shopping complex north of Murramarang House opened in the late 1980s. It now contains a supermarket, butcher, bread shop, newsagency, estate agent, liquor store, fast food shop, hardware shop, gallery, hairdresser and doctor's surgery.

Camping areas and caravan parks have gradually replaced the uncontrolled bush camping of earlier years. Council put up 'No Camping' signs, reserved some areas for day picnickers only, and provided toilet facilities. The Kioloa camping area and caravan park was the earliest; it was started by Jack Kemp

9. RECENT DEVELOPMENTS

after World War II. The shop opposite the park entrance also dates from this period. Some people felt they were not treated well by Jack, accusing him of praying for rain then charging for pulling them out of bogs with his blitz buggy.

John and Jean Brierley started the caravan park behind the south end of Racecourse Beach in the mid-1960s, on 146 acres of land. This block is the part of block D (see Map 1) east of the Bawley Point–Kioloa road. It had not been developed previously, so they began with virgin bush. The work was hard; they had four children between the ages of two and eight when they started. There was a drought in the early years, so water supply was a serious problem, solved only by refurbishing a well in the north end of their property. The water was excellent, and they were able to truck some of the water to local residents. Their van park was called 'Camp Nundera', but the name was changed recently to 'Racecourse Beach Tourist Caravan Park'.

Brian Wallace began the caravan park at Pretty Beach around 1960, and Stan Bogle started another one at Merry Beach some years later. This was initially north of the creek, but was later extended south of the creek by Brian Wallace. After Murramarang National Park was gazetted, the NPWS wanted to close the van park at Pretty Beach, but was persuaded to change its mind.

Dune stabilisation was carried out by the Soil Conservation Service during the past 20 years. The main areas treated were Racecourse Beach, Gannet Beach, the midden area on Wilford's Point, and Bawley Point Beach. They may have been overzealous in this work. The character of the midden area has been completely changed, and users of the picnic area at Bawley Point cannot see much of the beach. [4]

Bush fires have always been a problem in this area. In the earlier years, it was up to individuals to fight the fires with anything that came to hand, as there was no special equipment, nor any organisation or training. Wet sacks or green boughs were used to beat the flames out; back-burning was also used.

---

4   The stabilisation work on the headland was done by NPWS, to protect the midden from further erosion. The vegetation now protects this very important site (A.G. and S.F.).

Figure 55: The Avenue, Kioloa, 1976.
Source: The Edith and Joy London Foundation of The Australian National University.

Volunteer fire brigades were started first at Kioloa then at Bawley Point, and many who lived locally and knew the area well gave much of their spare time over the years. Windsor Evans was Captain at Kioloa 1939–68, and Neil Evans gave excellent service there later, for the very long period of 43 years. Bill Fuller, who was running the guest house at Bawley Point, started the fire service there. Charlie Antill was Fire Captain at Bawley Point for many years. The proper buildings for storage of equipment are very recent.

Through luck in earlier years, and the efforts of the brigades later, there has been little damage to property from bush fires. I do not recall any family's house being destroyed by bush fire since 1920, but three houses and some farm buildings were burnt at Termeil in the 1890s. One of the worst fires was in 1939, when the area from Termeil to the coast was burnt out. My grandmother described the scene after this fire: 'You could chase a mouse from Termeil to Bawley Point and not lose it once!' And I recall a massive stranding of insects along the beaches; they had been blown out to sea by the hot westerlies that accompanied a fire, and washed ashore by a north-easter a day or so later, some still alive. The destruction of Kioloa mill around 1928 was due to a bush fire.

Permanent residents in the area are mainly either retirees, or engaged in service industries: teachers, builders, plumbers, electricians, painters, tilers, upholsterers, shopkeepers. The guest house provides some seasonal employment. The Edith and Joy London Foundation employs a manager, who runs the cleared part of the foundation as a farm, maintains foundation buildings and attends to the needs of visitors to the foundation. The only industry exploiting local materials is the removal of sand from the back of the north end of Racecourse Beach. This started around 1970, when John and Jean Brierley had the land. Initially, it was planned to treat the sand, which is finer than average, and use it for moulds for casting metals, but this plan was abandoned. It is now used for general building purposes. In Jean Brierley's view, this activity is redressing an imbalance due to overgrazing in earlier years, which led to the dunes becoming mobile and covering previously useful land, including a small lagoon (Abraham's Lagoon). I recall the backs of the dunes being much nearer the shore, and certainly active (moving inland), in the 1920s.

Shortly after World War II there had been a flurry of excitement about mining the local beaches for rutile, and some claims were staked, much to the worry of the few local residents. This mining did not go ahead; apparently iron in the sand made processing too expensive.

Timber-getting, once the main local industry, has practically ceased. Don Baxter still operates a sawmill at Monkey Mountain, Termeil. Another mill back of Murramarang (block H on Map 1), started some decades ago by Charlie Mison, operated until around 1985. Brian Wallace was still cutting pit props about a year ago.

Figure 56: Baxter's sawmill, Termeil, 2015.
Source: Margaret Hamon, courtesy of the Baxter family.

THEY CAME TO MURRAMARANG

The year 1991 saw the opening of the Kioloa–Bawley Point Community Centre. This was financed partly by City of Shoalhaven, and partly by funds raised by the local Sports and Recreation Club, of which Wendy Montgomery was President and Bronwyn Clarke Secretary.

In the 1950s and earlier there was no provision for garbage collection. People either buried their garbage, dumped it in the sea, or took it out of the area. The nearest tip was at Ulladulla. Around 1965 council opened a local tip opposite the Racecourse Beach camping area. Around 1990 this was upgraded to a 'Refuse Transfer Station': you can dump your rubbish there in designated bins, which are whisked away out of the area at regular intervals, so reducing the smells and vermin associated with the earlier open trench system. Collection of recyclable items was also provided for. A system for weekly collection of household garbage from individual homes was also started around the same time.

Council has never provided a night soil collection service. In early years pit toilets were used, or cans which were emptied into the sea. I've been told part of one headland at Kioloa, used for this purpose, was known locally as 'Dunnican Point'. At present all residences and camping areas use septic tank systems. Council provides a pump-out service where there is not sufficient natural soil cover for absorption trenches, for example on Bawley Point itself. This service is not free. Generally, this system is working well, though some warnings of health risks and possible long-term damage to wetlands have appeared, for example in the 1980 dissertation by Williams.[5]

Residents and visitors rely on tank water for the most part, though some use is made of groundwater accessed by spear pumps. Kioloa camping area uses roof water for drinking, and dam water for showers, laundry and toilets. The guest house has frequent deliveries of water by road tanker during the summer season. There are no plans for a reticulated water supply, or for a sewerage system. The majority of residents feel these amenities would be too expensive.

I have enjoyed writing this book. It has brought back and refreshed many memories; old friendships have been renewed and new ones made. In the immediate future, Kioloa and Bawley Point will continue to cater mainly for tourists and retirees. The two villages have attracted people who like the peace

---

5 Williams, G. *An Environmental Study of the Coastal Strip from Bawley Point to Pretty Beach*, Bachelor of Architecture Dissertation, NSW Institute of Technology, 1980, p. 154.

and beauty of natural areas. There is always a threat that too much 'people pressure' on natural areas will destroy the very qualities which attracted people to the areas. Only continued vigilance will keep that threat in check.

EPILOGUE

MURRAMARANG IN THE EARLY TWENTY-FIRST CENTURY

Alastair Greig and Sue Feary

Bruce Hamon's book, *They Came to Murramarang*, provides a vivid account of the isolation that communities at Murramarang experienced over much of their post-settlement history, as well as the impact made by various forms of industry, communication and transportation in linking the area to the rest of the state, the nation and the world. The time that has elapsed since Bruce published the book in 1994 presents an opportunity to reflect on the pace of contemporary change in the area and the likely nature of future development.

Bruce's history of the area was published following a decade of significant population expansion during the 1980s. Between 1986 and 1991, the population of Bawley Point had grown from 261 to 433 people. Kioloa was not listed as a bounded locality for census purposes until 1996, when it recorded a population of 148 residents. In the intervening period since Bruce wrote his book, a returnee entering Bawley Point over the bridge at Willinga Lake, or entering Kioloa over the Butler's Creek bridge, would notice that the residential subdivisions had filled in and that the new homes are larger than their predecessors. Otherwise, they would have little difficulty recognising the area.

The 2011 census records that Bawley Point's population had risen to 591 people, while 208 residents lived at Kioloa and Merry Beach. Over the previous decade to 2011, Bawley Point had grown by 15 per cent, while Kioloa had grown by 5.1 per cent. These communities marking the northern and southern extremities of the area still retain a high proportion of holiday home owners, with both Bawley Point and Kioloa possessing more private dwellings than residents (687 and 304 dwellings respectively). At Bawley Point, 62.6 per cent of homes are listed as 'unoccupied private dwellings', while 66.2 per cent of dwellings at Kioloa share this status. However, during the summer period, between 10,000 and 15,000 people visit the area.

The demographic characteristics of the local population also reveal that the area remains popular for retirees. While the Australia-wide proportion of persons aged 65 or over in 2011 was 19.6 per cent, 39.1 per cent of residents at Bawley Point and 46.3 per cent of residents at Kioloa were 65 years or older. Furthermore, the area contains twice the number of outright home owners as the nation as a whole. Only 39.6 per cent of residents at Bawley Point and 29.6 per cent of people at Kioloa reported being in the labour force. In 2011, of those in the labour force, 18.6 per cent of residents at Kioloa and 9.3 per cent at Bawley Point listed 'accommodation' as their industry of employment, compared to an Australia-wide proportion of 1.2 per cent.

Demand for holiday accommodation (mainly from the Sydney–Illawarra region, but also from the Canberra region) remains strong, and has been serviced partly through the growth of small to medium-sized family-owned guest houses as well as bed and breakfast accommodation, near the beaches and in the bush west of Murramarang Road. Bruce's mother's guest house, the Bawley Point Guest House, closed down in 2001. While the original Californian bungalow–style house still stands — having finally served as the restaurant for the guest house — the spacious block has been subdivided gradually over the past 20 years to accommodate six other residential units.

The area also abounds with holiday rental properties but has not attracted large-scale resort complexes or hotels. Indeed, the 2012–17 Shoalhaven Tourism Master Plan acknowledges the value of Murramarang's present ambience, and lists as a desired outcome that the area be 'recognised as one of the special, treasured areas on the South Coast, providing the quintessential coastal village experience'. The Bawley Point Kioloa Community Association also performs an active role in keeping the community informed of developments that have the potential to change the character of the area.

The four on-site caravan parks that Bruce described (at Racecourse Beach, Kioloa, Merry Beach, and Pretty Beach) have been reduced to three, after NSW National Parks and Wildlife Service ordered the removal of the on-site Pretty Beach caravans at the turn of the millennium. The NPWS Plan of Management for Murramarang National Park, formulated in 1997, identified that most of the caravan sites were permanently occupied by private holiday vans. This placed restrictions on other park users, such as day visitors, campers and short term/

casual van stays. In these circumstances, the National Parks and Wildlife Act requires facilities to be offered across the recreational use spectrum. The subsequent redevelopment plan required permanent holiday vans to be phased out over a five-year period.[1] The other caravan parks remain popular holiday resorts in high season, while the Racecourse Beach caravan park also possesses a dedicated, gated residential park.

As a critical mass of permanent residents has grown in the Murramarang area, the scale and location of retailing has evolved. For much of the post–World War II period, holidaymakers and locals relied on the fibro-clad convenience store adjacent to the Kioloa caravan park on Murramarang Road. The store grew incrementally over the years, catering for the seasonal influx of tourists, and assumed the role of the local petrol station and fish and chip shop. The centrality of this location for the area was enhanced by the nearby establishment of the local fire depot and tennis courts. However, by 2014, shopping in the Murramarang area had become more bifurcated. A couple of years before Bruce's book was published, a shopping centre was built off Voyager Drive on the outskirts of Bawley Point to meet the needs of the locals, who had previously relied on Kioloa or Termeil service station for convenience goods. In the heart of Bawley Point, the Bawley Point Café has also developed a casual dining clientele. At the other end of the Murramarang settlement at Merry Beach, Kioloa, the new subdivisions encouraged the establishment of a restaurant attached to the convenience store on Merry Street. These retailing and dining enterprises servicing permanent residential and holiday demand took custom away from the original Kioloa store, which closed down in the mid-2000s. However, the store reopened in 2015.

Bawley Point and Kioloa are becoming unique communities with respect to the provision of other services. For example, the area is one of the few along the coast yet to be connected with mains water and mains sewerage. Shoalhaven Council has extended mains sewerage as far south as Lake Tabourie (just under 10 kilometres north of Bawley Point as the crow flies), but Murramarang remains reliant on water tanks for potable water and septic tanks for waste. Older 'absorption' septic systems are being replaced with 'pump-out' systems, reducing some of the pressure on ground soil. Mobile phone services remain unreliable and it is estimated that it will be a number of years before the area is connected by the National Broadband Network. Furthermore, most school-aged residents within the area still attend schools in Ulladulla, some 30 kilometres

---

1   NPWS, *Murramarang National Park, Brush Island Nature Reserve, Belowla Island Nature Reserve and Tollgate Islands Nature Reserve Plan Of Management*, NPWS, Sydney, 2002.

north. Consistent with the demographic profile noted earlier, only 17.2 per cent of Bawley Point's population and 13.9 per cent of Kioloa's population were under 20 years of age in 2011, compared with 25.8 per cent Australia-wide.

As Bruce's book documented, William Walker's homestead on 248 hectares, cleared and developed just north of the Kioloa sawmill before World War I, was eventually purchased by Edith and Joy London in 1929. While Joy remained at this property until her death in 1995, she had earlier bequeathed it to The Australian National University, under a 1975 deed of gift whereby ANU would maintain the property (including its forest, cleared farmland, buildings and beach area) in its present condition for educational and research purposes. In the subsequent 20 years, ANU fulfilled this commitment, and added a number of buildings to ensure its functionality as a university coastal campus.

However, in the late 1990s, ANU management undertook a series of budgetary measures designed to reduce costs, and questioned whether maintaining the Kioloa campus was part of its 'core business'. A proposal to divest itself of responsibility for the property was challenged by a concerted campaign by many members of the ANU community, spearheaded by its Kioloa Management Committee. The issue was resolved when the new Vice-Chancellor, Professor Ian Chubb, visited Kioloa in 2001 and was impressed enough with the site to commit the university to enhancing the status of the campus as one of the world's foremost coastal academic field stations. Since then, the Kioloa coastal campus has upgraded its existing buildings — including its heritage-listed homestead, timber-workers' cottages, and old schoolhouse — and placed the station on a self-financing footing. In 2012, it erected a new $3 million multi-purpose building that was officially opened with a smoking ceremony and welcoming address conducted by local Indigenous elders. It boasts a theatre hall with a capacity for 150 people, breakout rooms, a service area and a display room holding the African artefacts collected by Joy London's father.

Apart from aiming to provide ANU students from all natural and social sciences disciplines with a research experience at Kioloa, the campus hosts highly popular annual open days for the general public during the first week in January, showcasing the campus and the research of ANU academics. ANU has also dedicated part of a paddock to a highly successful community garden supported by over 80 local residents, and maintains a dedicated program to protect the critically endangered Hooded Plovers that inhabit its shoreline. The open fields of the campus also act as an important firebreak for the community of Kioloa.

Over the past two decades, the Murramarang region has inspired research by people from many different disciplines and walks of life, and this research complements Bruce's history. Archaeologist Michael Tracey spent years corresponding with Bruce about the history of the local timber industry, as he was interested in trying to match the archaeological record with information derived from archives and oral history. In 1994 he submitted an honours thesis on the archaeological expression of timber-getting, timber transport, and shipbuilding in the Murramarang district, which involved research on land and in the ocean. His research led to the discovery of some fascinating maritime archaeology in the ocean depths below Bawley Point. Tracey later published research on the ship the SS *Douglas Mawson*, built and launched from Bawley Point in 1914 and mentioned in Bruce's book.

Tracey's question of whether the timber tramways associated with the Kioloa and Bawley Point sawmills were ever linked remains pertinent today. Since 2011, after retiring from his Batemans Bay-based position with Forestry Corporation of NSW (formerly the NSW Forestry Commission), Ian Barnes has explored the state forests looking for the remains of the timber tramways from a forester's perspective. While little remains of Guy's sawmill at Bawley Point, he discovered further evidence of the timber tramway that served it. Barnes and another forester, Ian Bevage, have plotted kilometres of the tramways accurately onto topographic maps.

Ulladulla-based historian Cathy Dunn has researched the convict history of Murramarang and in 2006 published *Masters and Convicts: Murramarang and Ulladulla*. This manuscript contains an index of Milton and Ulladulla and other South Coast church records, cross referenced with civil registrations. It presents lists of convicts and the farms and estates in the district to which they were assigned, and the names of their masters, including Sydney Stephen, William Morris, and later William Carr at Murramarang.

The Murramarang area that Bruce describes is situated in the natural environment of the South Coast, whose beauty and 'naturalness' have been a draw card for visitors and residents for decades. Keeping it that way has not been easy. Despite its isolation — perhaps because of its isolation — Bawley Point and Kioloa remain attractive villages. Since the early 1990s, there has been no major subdivisional development for residential purposes, and few vacant blocks now remain on the two subdivisions on either side of Forest Road on the edge of Murramarang National Park that were cleared around the time Bruce wrote his book. Larger blocks of land closer to the bush behind Bawley Point have also been developed and a range of entrepreneurial ventures have been established in accommodation, equestrian activities, horticulture and viticulture between Bawley Point and Termeil. Unless more residential land is 'unlocked', people looking to settle or erect holiday homes in the area will compete for the existing limited resources. Shoalhaven Council's Tourism Master Plan also suggests that any future development in the area would have to remain consistent with the existing social and natural environment.

The area also has been afforded natural protection from development, being bounded by Murramarang National Park to the south, state forests to the west, Meroo National Park and lakes to the north, and the Tasman Sea to the east. The Murramarang Aboriginal Area also affords protection from development between Bawley Point and Racecourse Beach. The commitment by ANU to preserve its site in its current and natural state also removes Joy London's fear that her property would be subdivided for residential purposes.

Along with the socioeconomic changes in the Murramarang region since Bruce wrote this book, there have been major government initiatives to improve protection of Australia's marine and forest biodiversity. The Southern Regional Forest Agreement was one of several agreements between State and Federal governments to find a balance between conserving native forests and extraction of timber for saw logs and woodchips. Controversial, prolonged and often acrimonious, by 2001 the Southern Regional Forest Agreement had delivered an extension to Murramarang National Park on the eastern side of the Princes Highway and created new protected areas — Meroo National Park and Barnunj State Conservation Area. These were subsequently combined to create the 4,000-hectare Meroo National Park between Burrill Lake in the north and Bawley Point in the south. This national park protects the catchments of a suite of significant wetlands and coastal lakes, provides camping and other recreational opportunities and conserves landscapes rich in cultural heritage. including Indigenous sites and evidence of early timber production.

Equally controversial was the creation of Batemans Marine Park in 2006. Formulation of the Marine Parks Act in 1997 was the NSW government's response to global concerns over dwindling fish stocks and inadequate protection of marine ecosystems. The Marine Parks Act allows for sustainable fishing but does include 'no-take' sanctuary zones.

Batemans Marine Park covers 85,000 hectares of the Tasman Sea, between Bawley Point in the north and Wallaga Lake in the south, and extends from mean high water mark to three nautical miles offshore, where it adjoins Commonwealth waters. The marine park contains numerous lakes and estuaries and several offshore islands. Many people robustly opposed the creation of the marine park but much of this was fuelled by a misunderstanding of the perceived constraints on fishing. Some commercial fisher livelihoods were affected, but they received compensation for their hardship. Recreational fishing is deeply embedded in the Australian psyche and the community is divided in its views on the marine park. The NSW Liberal government currently has an amnesty on recreational fishing in some sanctuary zones and a moratorium on any new marine parks. We are yet to see whether this has been a wise decision but it shows that finding a balance between conservation and sustainable use is essential if humans want to share their South Coast environment with all of life's biodiversity.

EPILOGUE

Due to these social, economic, regulatory and geophysical circumstances, there is ample reason to hope that the Murramarang area that Bruce so eloquently described will be preserved for future generations. Yet, this epilogue can only echo Bruce's final warning that 'only vigilance' will keep in check the threat to the area's attractions. At the jetty on the north of O'Hara Head, two concrete blocks — remnants of the old Kioloa sawmill — are slowly being reclaimed by sand and vegetation. As these remaining visual landmarks disappear, the region can be even more grateful for Bruce's vivid description of the history of Murramarang.

INDEX

Aboriginal people, 1
    arrival, xxvii–xxix
    Batemans Bay Local Aboriginal land
        Council, xxxii
    burial grounds, xxx–xxxi, 110, 129
    burning, xxxi
    ceremonial activities, xxxii
    timber industry, 73
    food, xxx, 21, 73
    frontier conflict, 11–3
    middens, xxvii, xxx, 1, 15, 128, 129,
        136, 139
    Murramarang Aboriginal Area, 1, 5,
        136, 150
    significant sites, xxix
    tools, xxxi
aircraft landings, 103, 126
Allman, Captain, 12–3
Andrews, Captain, 80, 90
Andrews, Pross, 52, 129
Anthony, Michael, 88, 114
Antill, Charlie, 140
Australian National University, The, xxiv,
    xxv, xxxiii, 25, 120, 135–8, 148, 150
Avenue, The, 54–5, 62, 89, 115–6, 120,
    124, 129, 133, 138, 140

Backhouse, Bob, 64
Bailey, Mrs, 123
Barclay's Harbour (Kioloa), 19
Barnes, Ian, 149
Bass, George, 4

Batemans Bay, xxii, 5, 11, 32, 36, 38, 68,
    83, 84, 136, 149
Batemans Marine Park, 150
Bawley Point survey, 39
Baxter, Arthur, 60
Baxter, Olive (née Hapgood), 26
Beadman family, 68, 92, 110
Beattie, Mr, 54, 64
Belowla Island, 74
Benandra, 49, 110
Bendalong (Redhead), 36, 48, 60, 133
Bennett, Jack, 52, 129
Berrymann, Joseph, 12–3, 16
Bevage, Ian, 149
Bevan, Jack, 85, 117
Bevan, Mrs Ena (née Hogg), 64, 79, 121
Blackburn and Sons, 32, 88, 101
Boag, Mrs W. (née Annie McDonald), 56
Boiler, The, xxxv, 63, 84
Books, Captain, 73–4
Bowman, Dr D., 98
Braidwood, 5, 20, 63, 82, 117, 125
Brierley, John and Jean, 139, 141
Brooman, 17, 20–1, 22, 26, 30, 49, 50, 56,
    82, 83, 84, 124
Broulee, 5, 30, 72
Browne, Heather, 48, 129
Browne, Henry, 43, 125
Brush Island, xxiv, 1, 2, 3, 4, 10, 14, 17,
    59, 67, 74, 75, 77, 127, 136
Bucholtz, Mr and Mrs Fred, 123
Bull Pup Beach, 11, 74, 75–6

Bundle property, 24, 120
Burrill Lake, xxviii, 1, 4, 24, 29, 30, 57, 59, 81, 86, 103, 150
bushfires, 24, 81, 140, 148
Butler, L. W. (Sonny), 2, 117
Butler, Tom, 116–7
Butler's Creek, 26, 117, 145
Butler's Point, xxxvi, 73, 117

Cambage, R. H., 5
camping, 96, 98, 107, 116, 150
camping and caravan parks, 138, 142, 146–7
Carr, William, xxxvi, 7, 9, 14, 15, 19–20, 135, 149
Carriage family, 75
    Carriage, Frank, xix, 75, 96, 122
cattle, xxxvi, 9, 10, 11, 13, 17, 24, 68, 92, 120,
caves, Durras Mountain, 32, 110–1
Chaseling, William, 55
Chin Slin, 93
Chubb, Proffesor Ian, 148
Clyde Mountain, 5
Clyde River and valley, 36, 74, 83, 104
coach services, xxiii, 82, 86
Collins family, 60, 83, 91, 94, 127
    Collins, Reg and Innes, xxiv, 74, 91, 92, 110, 126
Community Centre, 142
Community garden, 148
convicts, 5, 10–1, 15, 149
Cook, Captain, 3–4
Cooley family, 116
Coomee (Aboriginal woman), 2
Cormack, Mr and Mrs P., 123
Cormorant Beach, 56, 110
Creer, Jack, 117
Cullen family, 112
    Cullen, Bill, xxiv, 57, 59, 73, 110
    see also Mison, Mrs N.
Cunningham, Andrew, 103

dairying, 17, 18, 28–9, 31, 66, 68, 121, 130
Dauphin map, 3
Dent, Dr Owen, xxiv, 15

depression of 1890s, 36, 39, 53
depression of 1930s, 40, 49, 59, 75, 104, 122
Drownings,
    Brown brothers, 75
    Lynn sisters, 69
Duncan, Syd Lewis, 75
dune stabilisation, 1, 3, 139, 141
Dunn, Cathy, 149
Durras Mountain, xxiii, 5, 17, 29–30, 32, 58, 59, 60, 63, 83, 84, 88, 136
    farming and grazing on, 29–30, 58, 68, 88, 92

East Lynne, 49, 53, 94, 117
Edith and Joy London Foundation, (ANU), xxiv, 54, 65, 89, 135–41, 148
Ellis, A. and E. and family, 39, 40, 48, 77, 79, 97, 99
European exploration, 3–4
Evans family, 9, 23–34
    Evans Frank, 25–6, 85, 100, 130
    Evans John I, 23
    Evans John II, 23, 24, 27
    Evans, Neil, xxiii, 24, 25, 26, 29, 35, 40, 74, 85, 121, 126, 129–30, 136, 140
    Evans, Windsor, 25, 31, 130, 140

family life in 1920s, 113–4
fishing, 2, 91, 95, 97, 100, 133, 150
Flat Rock, xviii, 48–9, 54, 84, 87, 92, 94
Florance, Thomas, 4, 8, 19, 32
Forestry Commission of NSW, 51, 52, 86, 149
Froude, Lorna, xxiv
Fuller, Bill, 123, 140

Gannet Beach, 102, 126, 137, 139
garbage collection, 142
Garrad, Robert, 10, 11, 12, 16, 82
Gibbney, Jim, xxiv, 7, 71
Giddens, Captain, 72
Gleeson, Mrs, 65
Goodlet and Smith (sawmillers), 36–7, 55, 60, 62, 73
Green, Edward, 19

INDEX

Guesthouse at Bawley Point, xix, 89, 95–8, 107, 122–3, 146
Guy family, 9, 29, 38, 48, 57, 92, 120, 121
    Guy, Alan, 137
    Guy, Mrs N., 29, 38

Hamon family, 87–112
    Hamon, Alma, xvii–xviii, xxiii, xxv, xxxiii, 61, 81, 87, 89, 90, 94–6, 98, 122–3
    Hamon, Bruce, xvii–xix (early life), xix–xxii (career), xxii–xxv (retirement and writing), 87–112
    Hamon, Les, 87, 88, 89, 90, 100, 103, 122–3
    Hamon Margaret, xxi, 126
Hapgood family, 59, 92, 102, 103, 117
Haskins, Gerald, 97, 123
Hassell, Douglas, 121
Hayes, Mr A. B., 54, 100–1
Herne, Artie, 126
Hoddle, Robert, 5, 8
Hogg, Andrew, 117
holiday accommodation, 146
holidaymakers
    pre-World War II, 96–8, 107
    post-World War II, 138–9
    twenty-first century, 146–7
    Shoalhaven Tourism Master Plan, 146–9
Holman, J., 10
Holt, Tony, 74–5
hospital, 69

Illawarra and South Coast Steam Navigation (ISN) Company Limited, 80–1

Jackson, Captain, 80
Jarman, Mrs Grace (née Kellond), 76, 116, 123
Johnston, Ralph, 97, 109, 122

Kellett, Eliza, 55
Kellond family, 117, 123–4
    Kellond, Billy, 124
    Kellond, Marie, 121, 124
    see also Jarman, Mrs Grace

Kelly, Mr H. H., 103
Kemp, Jack, 138–9
King, Lucy, 37, 86
Kioloa surveys, 19–20, 32 (1843), 56–7 (1893)
Kiola Star (newspaper), 67

land grant procedure, 8
land ownership, xxxvi, 7–8, 9, 120–1
Land Rights Act, xxxii
land sub-division, recent, 135, 137–8, 149
Larmer, James, 19–21
Lau, Hermann, 30
Lees, Dr Brian, xxiv
Lemon Trees, The, 66
Logpaddock (Juwin) Headland, 35, 103
London, Joy, xxxiii, 25, 54, 60, 117–20, 130, 133, 135–7, 148
London, Mrs, 60, 117
London, Edith, 117–20, 135
Lowder, Jackey, 12
Lynn, John, 69

Macalister, Lt J., 11
Marine Parks Act, 150
marine survey, Bawley Point, 103
McDonald, Captain, 76
McInnes, Mr, 43
McKay's farm, 58, 68
McKenzie, Helen Mary, 61, 65
McKenzie, Hepburn, 37, 61, 65, 113
Meroo, 4, 29, 30–1, 57, 59, 81, 82, 83, 90, 91, 98
Meroo National Park, 150
Merry Beach, 35, 54, 93, 130, 138, 139, 145, 146, 147
Miles, Captain, 80
Milton, xviii, 5, 11, 23, 24, 32, 53, 62, 65, 69, 87, 88, 93, 94, 101, 104, 108, 113, 117, 121, 125, 126, 149
mining, 67, 68
    gold, 58–9
    sand, 141
    shellgrit, 59
Mison, Mrs N. (née Gladys Cullen), 129
Mitchell, George, 117
Moore family (earlier family), 80, 113–6

155

Moore, Alice, 113–4
Moore George, 26, 37, 47, 48, 50, 74, 113–5, 126
Moore, Robert, 113–5
Moore family (later family), 117–9, 135
    Moore, Bernice (Bobbie), 60, 117, 124
    Moore, Humbert, 25, 117–9
    Moore, Mr Edward, 117–8, 135
    Moore, Mrs Kate, 117, 135
Morris, William Turney, xxxvi, 5, 7–15, 35, 149
Moruya, 11, 15, 26, 71, 84, 86
motor vehicles, 48, 49, 63, 84, 87, 88, 118
Mt Edgecombe property, 9
Murramarang
    earliest European settlement, 7–15
    the Carr era, 15–22
    the Evans era, 23–35
    the Timber era, 35–70
    end of the timber era, 87–134
    post-war era, 135–151
    1829 survey, 5
    1837 notice of sale, 17
    1841 census, 16
    1843 survey, 19, 21
    Ann Rees Jones description, 20
    1863 inventory, 28
    Town and Country Journal report, 30–2
    electoral roll (1922), 132–3
    census of dwellings, 136 (1964–1993), 145–6 (2011)
    census of population 2011, 145–6
    geology, xxvii–xxviii
    lagoon, 4, 5, 10, 14, 59, 91, 110, 126, 129
    Murramarang House, 10, 14, 16–9, 23–5, 28, 29, 62, 76, 121, 124, 138
Murramarang National Park, xxx, 2, 24, 136, 139, 146–7, 149–50

Nelligen, 32, 68, 83, 84, 113, 125
Nicholson, Jack, 14
Nuggan Headland, 40, 92
Nundera Point, xxx, 59, 139

O'Hara Head, xxviii, 19, 35, 57, 74, 115, 124, 151

Orr, William S., 9, 24–5, 60, 76, 90, 93, 120–1, 124, 133
outrigger, 22, 28

Page, Billy, 44, 116
Parkes, Varney, 111
Peacock, William, 102,
Pearson, William, 36, 55, 67
peat deposits, 110
Pebbly Beach, xxiii, xxxvi, 38, 48, 113, 124
Pigeon House Mountain (Didthol), xxxii, 2, 3, 4, 59, 104
place names, origins, 4, 32
postal services, 60–1, 94, 130
Pretty Beach, 100, 114, 136, 139, 146

'Queensland Gates', 86

rabbits, xxiv, 10, 17, 100
rabbitting, 91, 93, 100–1, 110, 114
Racecourse Beach, 3, 15, 129, 141, 142, 146, 147, 150
radio, 64, 93, 119
Rees Jones family, 20, 30, 82, 83
Reynolds, Henry, 85, 104, 106, 107
Reynolds, Mary (Broda), xxiii, 85, 97, 104–11, 122, 127, 140
Ritchie, Robert, 24
roads, 5, 11, 32, 48–9, 53, 69, 81–6, 118
    Bawley Point–Termeil, 63, 84, 85, 136
    Clyde Mountain Road, 5
    Durras Mountain, 56, 63
    Kioloa, 24, 84, 85
    Milton–Termeil, 62, 67, 84
    Monkey Mountain Road, xviii, 54, 56, 84,
    Murramarang–Batemans Bay, 83
    Murramarang–Brooman, 30, 82, 83
    Murramarang–Ulladulla, 17, 29–30, 30–1, 81, 83
    Murramarang Road, 136, 146, 147
    Nowra–Bega, 85
    'Old Coach Road', xxiii, xxiv, xxv, xxvi, 81–2, 84, 11
    Princess Highway, 84
    Smart's Road, 53, 84
    state forest rods, 85

Woodburn, 84
sawmills, 28, 32, 35–52, 73
    Bawley Point, xviii, 38–42, 43–4, 45–7, 64, 149
    Baxter's, 49, 141
    Benandra, 49
    Bridge Creek, 49
    Brooman, 49
    Coramba, 37, 113
    Flat Rock, 48–9
    Kioloa, 36, 37–8, 44–5, 47, 60, 64, 67, 151
    McMillan's, 58
    Nelligen, 113, 123
    Pebbly Beach, 48
    pit-sawmill, 35
    'spot and swing', 49
    Redhead, 36
    Termeil mills, 49
Scheele, Peter, 47, 110
schools, xxiii, 33, 53, 136, 147–8
    Bawley Point, 54, 56, 57
    Brooman, 56
    East Lynne, 53
    Kioloa, 54, 55
    Murramarang, xvii, 54, 57, 100–2, 121, 123–4
    Pebbly Beach, 48
    Redhead (Bendalong), 36
    Termeil, xvii–xviii, 54–5, 56, 102
school bus service, 136, 147–8
school days in the 1920s, 100–2
Scott, Walter, 92, 94, 130–1
    Scott, Mrs, 54, 130
Settree, A. W. and family, 76–7, 79, 123
sewerage systems, 142, 147
sheep, 17, 24, 121
ships
    Agnes and Henry, 74
    Albion, 7
    Arab, 73
    Benandra, 80, 81
    Bergalia, 72, 80, 81
    Bermagui, 72, 80, 81
    Bonnie Dundee, 66, 72–3
    Bull Pup, 74
    Camden, 74

    Douglas Mawson, 39, 76–80, 123, 149
    Gleaner, 73
    Hilda, 73
    Industry, 71
    Lena Lillian, 58
    Mary Cosgrove, 74
    May Howard, 58
    Molinger, 73
    Narani, 72, 80, 81
    Northern Firth, 75–7, 118–9, 124
    Our Elise, 79
    Queen Bee, 51
    Samoa, 57, 73
    Sydney Cove, 4
    Waterwitch/Wonderwitch, 72
    Wee Clyde, 74
    Willlinga, 36
    Wyoming, 74
shipbuilding, 39, 76–80, 149
shipwrecks, xxxvi, 4, 72–7
Shoebridge, Mr (teamster), 43
shops, 88, 136, 138–9, 147 (see also Blackburn and Sons)
Simpson, Eric, 46, 49, 50, 132
skeletons at Murramarang, 126–30
Small, Bob, 117
social life in the 1890s, 67–8
South Durras, 30, 57, 58
Southern Regional Forest Agreement, 150
sport, 67–8, 115
Stephen, Alfred, 7
Stephen, Mr Justice, 7
Stephen, Sydney, 7–18, 20, 29, 35, 149
Stephens, Charlie, 26, 51, 57, 63, 65
Swan, Bert, 117
Switzer (Switzki), Gordon, 129
Sydney Cove survivors, 4

Tabourie, 1, 4, 14, 29–30, 57, 81–2, 84, 86, 147
Taylor, Nurse, 65
telephone services, 33, 43, 60–1, 76, 89, 94, 133, 147
Termeil, 4, 30, 32, 47, 54, 56, 66–7
Thompson, Hugh, 12–3
Thompson, Joe, 117

timber cutting and milling, 31, 35–52,
148–9 (see also sawmills)
    boiler cleaning, 50
  cedar, 35
  industrial deaths, 52
  'Joe' (work break), 49–50
  loading timber, 4–7
  pit props, 51, 141
  sleeper-cutting, 40, 50–1
  wages, 50, 58, 66
  working conditions, 49, 51–2
Tracey, Michael, 148–9
tramlines, xxxiv, 32, 42–4, 48–9, 57, 58, 66, 84, 86, 96, 118, 125, 149
trig station at Bawley Point, 59

Ulladulla, 2, 11, 17, 28, 29, 30, 32, 35, 49, 53, 58, 59, 62, 63, 74, 81, 82, 83, 88, 94, 121, 125, 133, 136, 142, 147, 149

Veitch, Mrs Lily (née Walker), 10, 25–6, 29, 57
Vider, Belle (née Walker), xxiv, 59, 62, 63, 64, 74, 81, 84, 85, 98, 103, 110, 116, 121, 127–9, 130,
Vider, Paul, 44, 125

Walker, Professor and Mrs D., 135
Walker, William and family, 9, 25, 26, 29, 60, 61–5, 74, 84, 87, 117, 120, 129, 130, 148
Wallace, Brian, 139
water supply, 139, 142, 147
wattle bark, 20–1
Watts, Dorothy, xxiv
wildlife, 110, 115, 148, 150
Wilford's Point, 15, 74, 129, 139
Willinga Lake Bridge, 42–3, 66, 84–5, 102, 125, 136, 145
Willinga Lake Crossing, 43, 81, 84–6, 102
Willinga property, 15, 24, 38, 83, 92, 121, 125, 137
Willinga settlement, 32, 60, 66
Willinga survey, 4
Wilson, Lindsay, 9, 57, 121
wine making, 20, 119, 149
Woondu breastplate, xxxiv–xxxv, 126–7

World War I, 64
World War II, 81, 133
worm-catching, 98, 114, 124
Wyld, Edward, 9, 120

www.ingramcontent.com/pod-product-compliance
Lightning Source LLC
Chambersburg PA
CBHW060930170426
43192CB00031B/2887